THE JEWELER'S DIRECTORY OF
Decorative Finishes

THE JEWELER'S DIRECTORY OF
Decorative Finishes

JINKS MCGRATH

krause publications

An Imprint of F+W Publications

700 East State Street • Iola, WI 54990-0001
715-445-2214 • 888-457-2873
www.krausebooks.com

A QUARTO BOOK

First published in North America in 2005
by Krause Publications
700 East State Street
Iola, WI 54990-0001

Library of Congress Catalog Card Number 2004116648

ISBN-13: 978-0-89689-193-7
ISBN-10: 0-89689-193-3

QUAR.JDF

Conceived, designed, and produced by
Quarto Publishing plc
The Old Brewery
6 Blundell Street
London N7 9BH

Project editor Jo Fisher
Art editor Sheila Volpe
Designer Tanya Devonshire-Jones
Photographer Paul Forrester
Text editor Diana Steedman
Picture researcher Claudia Tate
Proofreader Alison Howard
Indexer Diana LeCore
Assistant art director Penny Cobb

Art director Moira Clinch
Publisher Piers Spence

Note to the reader
Many jewelry-making materials are toxic and hazardous
if not handled carefully. Please study carefully the health
and safety information on page 8 and adhere to good
practice at all times. The author, publisher, and copyright
holder cannot be held liable if this advice is disregarded.

Color separation by Universal Graphics Pte Ltd,
Singapore
Printed by Star Standard Pte Ltd, Singapore

10 9 8 7 6 5 4 3 2

CONTENTS

Introduction

When I began to write this directory of decorative finishes, my first thought was whether I would be able to think of enough ways to create different and interesting surfaces to utilize the techniques I employ every day in my work. I need not have worried! Once it was agreed which techniques were to be included in the book, it was just a question of getting started on a delightful journey of discovery. I found new and unexplored ways to create distinctive finishes on the surfaces of copper, brass, silver, and gold.

The main body of the directory demonstrates fifteen different jewelry techniques that can be used to produce a variety of decorative surfaces. Each technique has been divided into three sections. In the first section the method is demonstrated, and the tools and materials needed are discussed. In the second section, samples that have been worked using the technique are displayed. A third, showcase section follows, showing finished work from the collections of jewelers who work with that particular technique. Many of these inspirational pieces combine more than one technique to achieve some exquisite surfaces.

Some finishes may prove more difficult to achieve than others but I hope I have suggested methods that will result in hours of pleasure rather than frustration. A little flexibility and creativity on the part of the jeweler is always required when developing new ideas. For example, patination calls for trial and error in its undertaking, as success with this finish can often depend on weather conditions, or the quality of sawdust or earth used, or the state of the metal. Other techniques, such as enameling, granulation, or inlay, are more time-consuming to perform than, for example, hammering or fusing.

Once you are ready to use your decorated surfaces to create pieces of jewelry, there are two points to keep in mind. First, if the decoration is to be made before fabrication of a piece of jewelry, consider the ease with which it can be cleaned and filed after soldering, without spoiling the surface. Second, if the decoration is achieved by patination or oxidization, ensure that no further heating will be necessary, otherwise the color may disappear at fabrication.

The most important lesson for me when preparing the demonstrations of the techniques and making the different samples, is that there is really no limit to one's creativity and to what means it can be put. The more techniques that can be combined to produce varied surface finishes, the richer the ideas become. It is worth experimenting with your ideas before committing them to actual pieces, as often something unanticipated will change the look of a piece.

It just remains for me to say that if your experiments do not match exactly the appearance in the photographs of the demonstrated techniques and samples, don't worry; that is not the point. It may well be that you have discovered something new, beautiful, and exciting.

JINKS MCGRATH

Health and safety

Jewelry-making is a surprisingly dusty and dirty occupation, and the use of bottled gases, flammable liquids, and caustic solutions means you should exercise caution if you intend to work in a home environment. Jewelry-making is not in itself a dangerous business or hobby, but careless use of the equipment and materials could lead to accidents. Always make sure you have a first-aid kit handy in case of minor cuts and burns, and having a small fire extinguisher close by would also be prudent.

Follow these sensible precautions to avoid accidents:

- Always work in well-ventilated, well-lit conditions.

- Turn off your gas torch at the bottle when you have finished using it to prevent leaks.

- Never store chemicals or flammable liquids in unmarked containers. Always keep them out of the reach of children, and preferably in a metal container in the coolest part of the room.

- Keep children and animals well away from the jewelry workshop.

- Tie long hair back and avoid wearing loose clothing that can easily become caught on equipment.

- Always follow manufacturers' directions when using chemicals, resins, and caustic solutions.

- Wear safety glasses when using high-speed polishing equipment and drills.

- Wear a dust mask when using polishing equipment and during any activity that generates airborne dust particles.

How to use this book

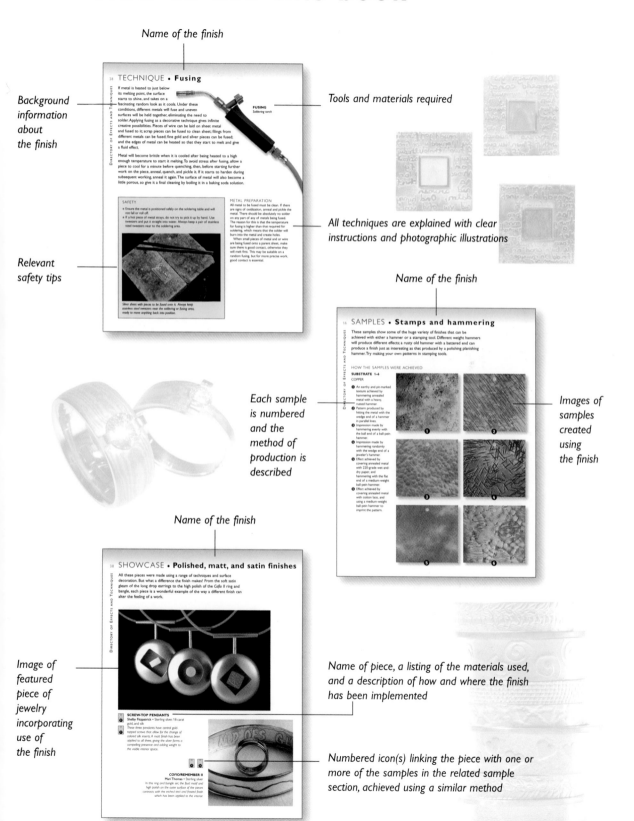

Name of the finish

Background information about the finish

Relevant safety tips

TECHNIQUE • Fusing

Tools and materials required

All techniques are explained with clear instructions and photographic illustrations

Name of the finish

SAMPLES • Stamps and hammering

Each sample is numbered and the method of production is described

Images of samples created using the finish

Name of the finish

SHOWCASE • Polished, matt, and satin finishes

Image of featured piece of jewelry incorporating use of the finish

Name of piece, a listing of the materials used, and a description of how and where the finish has been implemented

Numbered icon(s) linking the piece with one or more of the samples in the related sample section, achieved using a similar method

Essential skills

Note that the hottest part of the flame is at the tip of the inner of the two blue flames, about two-thirds down the length of the whole flame.

Choose the flame size according to the size of the piece being heated. Avoid using too small a flame.

ANNEALING

Annealing is the process of softening metal by heating it. Place the metal on a soldering table and play a gentle flame all over it. It is better to push the flame up and along a piece of metal rather than work across it. The surface of the metal will first oxidize, i.e. turn black, and then start to redden. Hold the metal at this dull red color for about 5 seconds, then turn off the heat. Allow the metal to cool for a few seconds before quenching and pickling it.

SOLDERING

Soldering is the joining together permanently of two or more pieces of metal. Clean the areas to be joined and ensure that the pieces will fit together closely.

Paint flux into and around the join. Place hard, medium, or easy solder paillons around the join using a small paintbrush or a pair of stainless steel tweezers. The paillons should be touching both pieces of metal. Introduce the flame slowly, as the water in the flux tends to bubble as it dries. After the flux has settled, turn up the heat of the flame and play it all around the two pieces of metal.

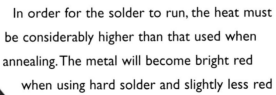

Strips and sheets of solder

In order for the solder to run, the heat must be considerably higher than that used when annealing. The metal will become bright red when using hard solder and slightly less red (and hot) when using medium or easy solder. When the solder runs, you will see a bright silver (or gold) line running through or around the join. Allow this to run for a second or two before removing the heat. Quench and pickle the piece.

Soldering torch

When soldering gold, the join must be very close (even closer than silver) and the paillons should be very small. Gold solder will not run in quite the same way as silver, so it is better to use more tiny paillons around the join than to try to solder with one or two large ones.

Use tweezers to plunge the metal into cold water.

QUENCHING

Quenching involves placing hot metal in cold water to rapidly cool it. After annealing or soldering, allow the metal to cool slightly before using either stainless steel or brass tweezers to place it into a container of cold water. The annealing and pickling of different carat golds can vary slightly; some may need to cool completely before quenching. Most suppliers will provide technical information as to how the different carats and colors of gold should be quenched.

PICKLING

Once a piece of metal has been annealed and quenched, it is usually pickled. Pickling removes oxide and residue flux, and cleans the metal. The most common pickling solutions are alum (two tablespoons to one pint of water), safety pickle (mixed as per the manufacturer's instructions), or a diluted sulfuric acid solution (one part sulfuric acid to ten parts water).

These solutions work faster if they are kept warm, either over an open flame as shown or in a plastic container sitting in water in an electric slow-cooker.

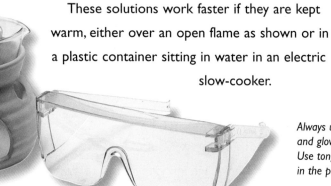

Always use safety glasses and gloves when pickling. Use tongs to place the piece in the pickling solution.

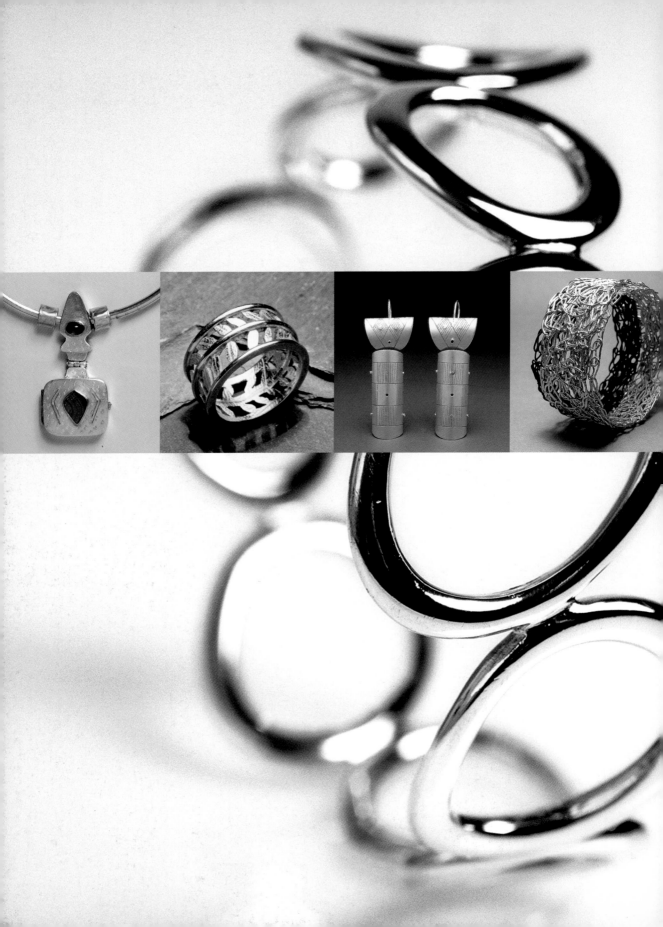

DIRECTORY OF
EFFECTS AND
TECHNIQUES

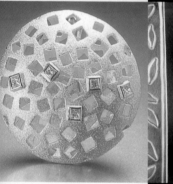

This directory of decorative finishes is a complete guide to the techniques, tools, and materials necessary to produce key surface effects for jewelry. From enameling to casting, and from granulation to etching, each finish is explained and illustrated to help you achieve the result you desire and to inspire you to experiment further.

Each finish is organized into three sections:

- A description of the techniques used to achieve the finish, with clear step-by-step instructions and a listing of the equipment needed

- A collection of different samples, demonstrating a range of variations on the finish with advice as to how each was completed

- An inspirational showcase of contemporary professional jewelry where some exciting and beautiful pieces have been created using the finish

TECHNIQUE • **Stamps and hammering**

Stamps are used to mark and shape metal to an exact pattern that has been cut in them. Commercially-produced stamps have a male and female pattern cut into hard steel by a professional "cutter" and may be incredibly detailed. Simple stamps can be purchased or made quite easily for small-scale use.

A hammered finish is often seen on large pieces of silverware, such as platters or candlesticks, and is the result of a piece being worked to achieve its shape. In jewelry making, metal can be hammered before or after fabrication.

Either end of a hammer will produce an interesting texture. The flat end, especially if it is old and marked, will produce a random texture. A ball-pein end will create a circular texture, and a wedge end will give thin or wide lines.

HAMMERS
① *Jeweler's hammer*
② *Wedge hammer*
③ *Ball-pein hammer*
④ *Planishing hammer*

STAMPS
⑤ *A variety of stamp ends*

MAKING A STAMP

"Tool steel" is required to make a stamp. It is available from ferrous metal suppliers in stock varying from $1/4$ inch/5mm square to $3/4$ inch/15mm round, depending on the size of stamp required. Have the stock cut into pieces 4 inches/10cm long.

❶ Heat the whole length of each 4 inch/10cm bar with a torch until it is cherry red. Allow it to air cool.

❷ File and cut the softened end into the desired pattern. The impression should stand proud as the background of the pattern is cut away.

❸ Reheat the whole length to a bright red and then quench it in water to harden. Check the pattern by hitting it into a lead "cake." Lead is softer than silver or copper and is better for showing a stamp mark. Refile or cut to adjust the shape as necessary.

❹ Polish the bar with wet-and-dry sandpaper and a polishing mop, paying attention to the patterned end as this makes it easier to see the color changes when tempering.

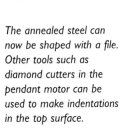

The annealed steel can now be shaped with a file. Other tools such as diamond cutters in the pendant motor can be used to make indentations in the top surface.

SAFETY

• When holding a piece of metal which is to be hammered, take care to keep fingers and thumbs away from the hammer. If necessary, leave an extra area that can be held tightly with a pair of pliers or a small handheld vice.

TEMPERING THE STAMP

Rub a little soap over the pattern to protect it. Heat the bar from the unpatterned end and watch the heat move toward the patterned end. Immediately a straw-yellow color appears, quench the bar in water or oil. Tempering makes the tool steel hard, but not brittle.

The tool steel is "tempered" to harden the working end. The heat for tempering is lower than the red heat needed to soften and work steel. This "bee's wing" effect is the color needed to ensure that the end will be hard enough.

USING THE STAMP

Place the metal to be stamped on the lead cake with a piece of leather, calico, or soft paper between it and the lead. Hold the bar at 90 degrees to the metal and use a hammer to hit the bar sharply to transfer the pattern onto the metal. A steel plate can also be used as a background support, but the metal should not be too thin or it will curl and harden up as the impressions are made.

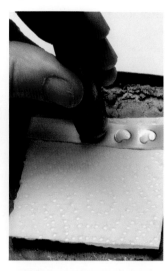

A lead cake is used to give a firm, but not too hard, surface, so that the punch can make an impression on the annealed silver. A double piece of paper is placed between the lead and the silver to avoid contamination.

HAMMERING

Whether hammering is done before or after fabrication, the technique is the same. For example, a plain ring may be easier if you make it first and then produce the texture. Its size will increase as the hammer action stretches the metal. This must be allowed for when measuring, or the ring should be sized correctly once hammering is complete.

The metal to be textured should be annealed and held on either a steel stake or a steel flatbed. There should be direct contact through the end of the hammer, the metal, and the steel stake. As the metal is worked it will become hardened, so if more texturing is required, anneal the piece again.

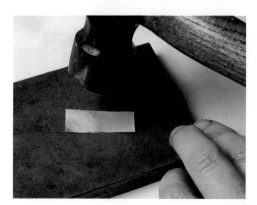

An old, rusty hammer from a blacksmith's workshop is hit flat against the silver to give random markings. Any dirt or oil should be cleaned away before further working is carried out.

The "ball" end of the hammer is used to mark the silver. This is done on a small steel plate as the marks do not need to be very heavy.

SAMPLES • **Stamps and hammering**

These samples show some of the huge variety of finishes that can be achieved with either a hammer or a stamping tool. Different weight hammers will produce different effects; a rusty old hammer with a battered end can produce a finish just as interesting as that produced by a polishing planishing hammer. Try making your own patterns in stamping tools.

HOW THE SAMPLES WERE ACHIEVED

SUBSTRATE 1–6

COPPER

❶ An earthy and pit-marked texture achieved by hammering annealed metal with a heavy, rusted hammer.

❷ Pattern produced by hitting the metal with the wedge end of a hammer in parallel lines.

❸ Impression made by hammering evenly with the ball end of a ball-pein hammer.

❹ Impression made by hammering randomly with the wedge end of a jeweler's hammer.

❺ Effect achieved by covering annealed metal with 220-grade wet-and-dry paper, and hammering with the flat end of a medium-weight ball-pein hammer.

❻ Effect achieved by covering annealed metal with cotton lace, and using a medium-weight ball-pein hammer to imprint the pattern.

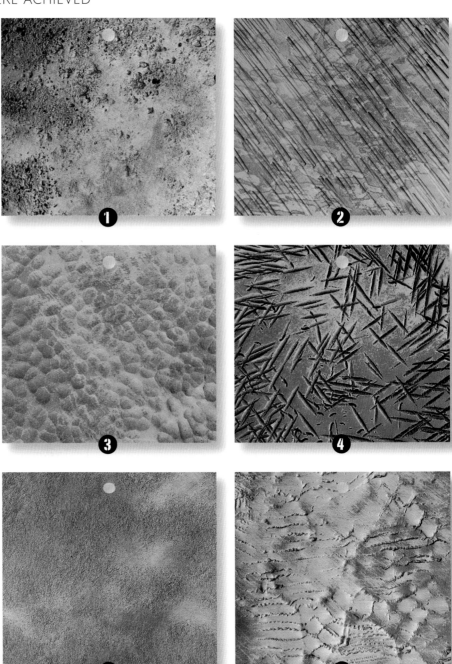

HELPFUL HINTS

- Always place the piece on a solid work surface, such as a steel plate or stake, a block of hard wood, or a lead cake.
- Try to hit the metal directly from above. When the hammer is at an angle, it makes deeper marks in the metal that are difficult to remove.
- Hammering metal hardens it. Remember to anneal the piece at regular intervals to keep it soft enough to work.
- When marking with a stamp, use a single sharp blow to avoid distorting the image.

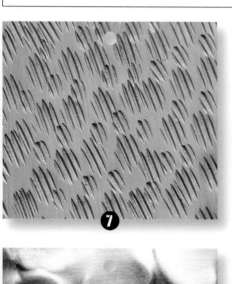

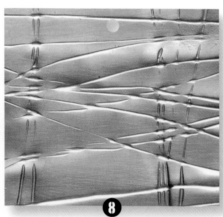

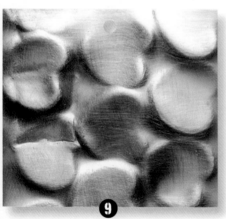

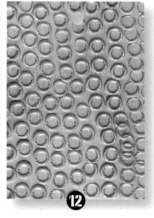

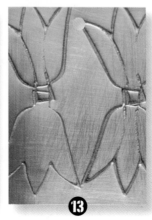

SUBSTRATE 7-13

SILVER

7 Effect achieved by applying a small, lined chasing tool evenly across annealed silver. The tool was hit with a medium-weight ball-pein hammer.

8 Silver annealed and wrapped with jeweler's binding wire, placed on a steel plate, and marked on both sides with the flat head of a hammer.

9 Imprint made on the reverse side of annealed silver with a heart shape made in the end of some steel stock.

10 Flower pattern formed in annealed silver using a small curved chasing tool to stamp the line markings.

11 Pattern produced using the wedge end of a small jeweler's hammer to mark horizontal and vertical lines to form cross-hatching.

12 Effect made by stamping a small chasing tool with a concave circular end in close strokes onto the annealed silver.

13 Flower shape formed end to end using a stamp pattern in the end of steel stock.

Before the advent of the rolling mill, all metal was hammered to shape and thin it. The considered marks of hammer work and handmade stamps are very beautiful; they indicate with great honesty how the shape was formed and the piece made.

WEDDING RINGS
Jonathan Swan • 18-carat yellow gold
These unusual wedding rings have been textured with a rusty hammer and stamped with punches to read "Love is blind" in Braille.

FUSED GOLD NECKLACE
Shelby Fitzpatrick • Sterling silver and 22-carat gold
Bold spirals of gold on inverted silver domes are alternated with discs that have been given a hammered texture.

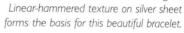

TOURMALINE LOCKET

Jinks McGrath • Sterling
silver and 18-carat gold with
tourmalines
*The body of this unique locket
has been made with silver, onto
which the pattern has been
stamped. The gold wires have
been fused onto the surface.*

MESH BRACELETS

Reinier Brom • Steel, copper, and brass
*These heat-oxidized bangles have been
hammered into shape and a rolling mill has
been used to give them their mesh texture.*

HAMMERED LEAF BRACELET

Shimara Carlow • Sterling silver and
18-carat gold
*Linear-hammered texture on silver sheet
forms the basis for this beautiful bracelet.*

TECHNIQUE • Rolling mill texturing

The surface of most metals can be transformed using a rolling mill. It's a relatively quick and easy process which is fun, while inviting plenty of invention and experimentation.

The rolling mill looks like a heavy-duty mangle, consisting of two polished hardened steel rollers. Although mills are unlikely to be the first purchase for the beginner, many jewelers will have access to this useful piece of equipment in colleges. The steel rolls can be flat for sheet metal, or grooved for wire, or patterned for decorating strips. The gap between the rollers can be adjusted so that sheet metal can be passed through under considerable pressure, in order to make it thinner. Although the traditional use for rolling mills is to make metal thinner, they are also useful for transferring almost any image or texture onto the metal surface. Do not try to reduce the thickness of the metal too rapidly as it may crack.

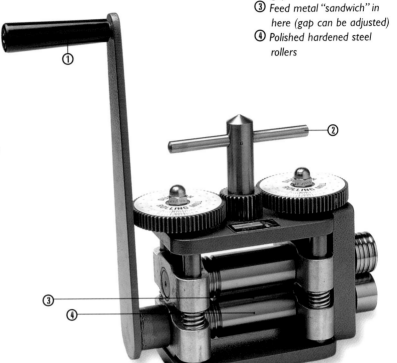

THE ROLLING MILL
① *Handle*
② *"T" handle used to adjust gap between rollers*
③ *Feed metal "sandwich" in here (gap can be adjusted)*
④ *Polished hardened steel rollers*

SAFETY AND CARE OF EQUIPMENT

- The rolling mill is a very safe tool, but you should always make sure it's properly secured to a sturdy work surface.
- Make sure your fingers don't get trapped between the rollers.
- When annealing, take care to avoid acid burns.
- Never use wet metal—the rollers will rust.
- Never use steel, titanium, sandpaper, or other tough materials that will damage the rollers, unless they are safely sandwiched between brass or copper.

PREPARING THE METAL

Anneal and clean the metal to be textured. Annealing your metal will make it malleable and soft, ready to take an impression. Metals such as copper, brass, silver, gold, or aluminum are all suitable. Platinum, white gold, nickel, and bronze are all too tough to achieve satisfactory impressions, and steel or titanium should never be used.

CHOOSING MATERIALS

Select the material to be used to impart texture, for example, watercolor paper, fabric, or organic material, such as a delicate feather, and so on, and cut to fit the metal surface. Experiment as much as you want, as the texture or pattern you use will define the nature of your finished piece. Do you want something subtle and textural or bold and dramatic? The possibilities of what you can use are almost limitless.

You can experiment with an endless variety of surfaces to achieve a wide range of embossed effects.

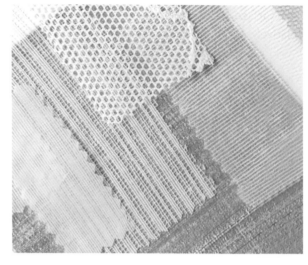

As you push down on the handle of the mill, you should meet some resistance.

USING A ROLLING MILL

❶ The rolling mill reduces the thickness of a sheet of metal as the sheet is passed through it. The "T" handle on the top is used to adjust the gap between the rollers. As the long handle is turned, the rollers pull the metal between them, compressing it slightly with each pass.

❷ You can also use a rolling mill to create pattern. With the two rollers tightened to the precise thickness of the metal sheet, most material will make an impression on it. Lace curtain material is particularly effective. Even something as fine as hair will make a significant impression on an annealed silver sheet. If you find that you have to bounce on the handle to make it move then you have set your gap too tightly. As a rough guide, you should be able to turn the handle with one hand but with difficulty. Always clean the rollers after use.

Here, aida, an evenly woven fabric with regularly spaced holes, was used to create a textured effect on silver.

A range of surface textures can be created, from delicate to heavily embossed.

SAMPLES • **Rolling mill texturing**

Here are just a few examples of the type of textures and patterns that you can achieve with this technique. As you can see, the process can be used for very subtle surface finishes as well as bold defining imagery. Where appropriate, a patina or oxide has been used to enhance the texture.

HOW THE SAMPLES WERE ACHIEVED

SUBSTRATE 1-9

COPPER

❶ Impression made using high-rag content, 320g watercolor paper.
❷ Impression made using fine brass mesh.
❸ Impression made using grade 4/0 garnet paper.
❹ Impression made using coiled and curved pieces of steel-binding wire.
❺ Impression made using lace from an old curtain.
❻ Impression made by passing a pierced steel template twice through the rolling mill, turning the template 90 degrees on the second passing.
❼ Impression made using crocheted linen.
❽ Impression made using lace fabric with flower pattern.
❾ Impression made using string.

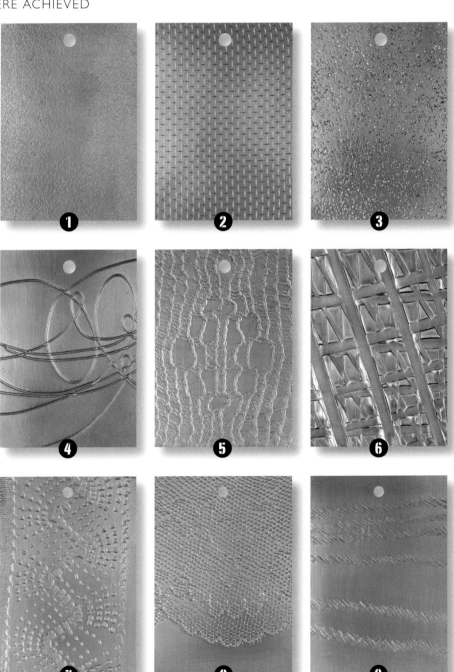

HELPFUL HINTS

- Don't over-tighten the rolling mill. This can flatten subtle textures such as paper and organic materials, or, with bold materials such as wire, cut through sheet metal.
- If you want to lay one texture over another, always start with the boldest texture.
- Allow for loss of subtle textures when forming and filing your metal into its finished form.

- When rolling two textures together at the same time make sure they are of a similar thickness, or one texture will detract from the other.
- Where necessary cut down high points on organic materials such as leaf stems and feather shafts.
- Ensure organic material is completely dry before rolling it.
- Rub your test pieces with a piece of wire wool. This will enhance subtle textures and brighten the metal.

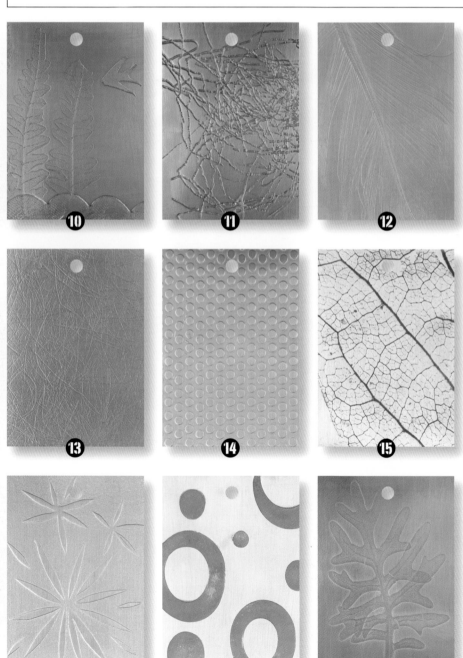

SUBSTRATE 10-11
COPPER

10 Impression made using a combination of different textures—dried leaf, cut paper, and braiding.

11 Impression made using scrunched and broken fine brass wire.

SUBSTRATE 12-14
BRASS

12 Impression made using a feather.

13 Impression made using Japanese paper.

14 Impression made using industrial perforated steel sheet.

SUBSTRATE 15-17
SILVER

15 Impression made using skeleton leaf, highlighted with a black oxide.

16 Impression made using a pattern cut out of watercolor paper.

17 Impression made using circle washer shapes and discs cut out of brass, then highlighted with cupric nitrate patina.

SUBSTRATE 18
GILDED METAL

18 Impression made using dried philodendron leaf.

SHOWCASE • **Rolling mill texturing**

The patterns and textures that you can transfer onto a piece of metal using a rolling mill are truly endless. From the smooth and precise effect achieved using watercolor paper, to the complete reproduction of steel mesh seen in the geometric necklace, the surfaces shown here demonstrate the diversity offered by this technique.

TEXTURED OR BANDED NECKLACE
Robert Feather • 18-carat yellow, white, red, green gold set with a sapphire
A subtle texture unifies the banded surface of the pendant.

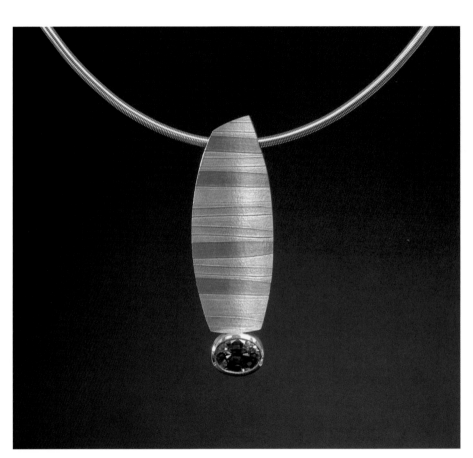

DOUBLE RING
Jinks McGrath • Sterling silver with 18-carat gold
Gold wire has been used to frame two large gemstones, surrounded by silver that has been textured with an open-weave fabric.

PIERCED RING

Jonathan Swan • 18-carat yellow gold
Leaf texture has been used to add subtle detail to this pierced band ring.

PATTERNED RINGS

Lisbeth Dauv • Sterling silver with 18-carat gold
In this collection of rings, the artist has used a range of materials to create patterns with the rolling mill. Fabric, mesh, and cut-paper textures on silver bands have been intersected with gold rings.

PATTERNED BELT

Georgina Taylor • Sterling silver, 18-carat gold, various gemstones, glass, and shell
This sumptuous piece has cleverly used a rolling mill to add pattern work with a paper template. The belt separates to form a necklace and two bracelets.

7 **14**

BEADED BRACELET
Jinks McGrath • Sterling silver, African amber, carnelian, and beads
For this colorful bracelet, some of the silver discs have been patterned through the rolling mill while fused gold and granulation have been added to others, enhancing the overall visual texture of the piece.

6

SPIRAL PATTERNED RINGS
Lisbeth Dauv • Sterling silver
Raised spirals decorate this simple band ring.

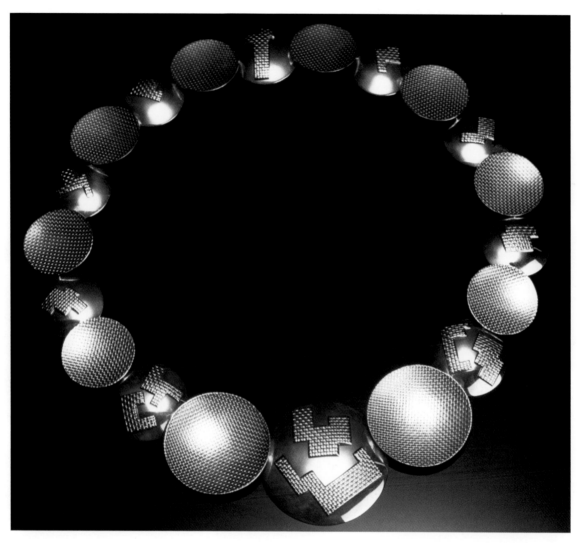

GEOMETRIC NECKLACE

Shelby Fitzpatrick • Sterling silver
*The units of this striking necklace have been
roller-printed with stainless steel mesh.
Textured geometric shapes have been applied
to alternate discs to create an effective
contrast within the piece.*

LEAF BROOCH
Robert Feather • 18-carat yellow,
white and green gold, tzavorite,
and diamond
*In this piece, the gold has been
rolled with watercolor paper to
produce this fine surface, which
has been offset with two
eye-catching stones.*

TECHNIQUE • Fusing

If metal is heated to just below its melting point, the surface starts to shine, and takes on a fascinating random look as it cools. Under these conditions, different metals will fuse and uneven surfaces will be held together, eliminating the need to solder. Applying fusing as a decorative technique gives infinite creative possibilities. Pieces of wire can be laid on sheet metal and fused to it; scrap pieces can be fused to clean sheet; filings from different metals can be fused; fine gold and silver pieces can be fused; and the edges of metal can be heated so that they start to melt and give a fluid effect.

FUSING
Soldering torch

Metal will become brittle when it is cooled after being heated to a high enough temperature to start it melting. To avoid stress after fusing, allow a piece to cool for a minute before quenching, then, before starting further work on the piece, anneal, quench, and pickle it. If it starts to harden during subsequent working, anneal it again. The surface of metal will also become a little porous, so give it a final cleaning by boiling it in a baking soda solution.

SAFETY

- Ensure the metal is positioned safely on the soldering table and will not fall or roll off.
- If a hot piece of metal strays, do not try to pick it up by hand. Use tweezers and put it straight into water. Always keep a pair of stainless steel tweezers near to the soldering area.

Silver sheet with pieces to be fused onto it. Always keep stainless steel tweezers near the soldering or fusing area, ready to move anything back into position.

METAL PREPARATION

All metal to be fused must be clean. If there are signs of oxidization, anneal and pickle the metal. There should be absolutely no solder on any part of any of metals being fused. The reason for this is that the temperature for fusing is higher than that required for soldering, which means that the solder will burn into the metal and create holes.

When small pieces of metal and or wire are being fused onto a parent sheet, make sure there is good contact, otherwise they will melt first. This may be suitable on a random fusing, but for more precise work, good contact is essential.

FUSING METAL

When fusing a metal to a contrasting metal, the differing melting temperatures will alter the way fusing occurs. With low-carat gold, particularly 9-carat, the temperature needs to be monitored carefully. If 9-carat gold becomes hotter than silver, it has a tendency to dissolve and spread into the silver.

If your piece is to be hallmarked, do not fuse silver or copper onto any gold and likewise, copper should not be fused onto silver.

APPLYING THE HEAT

❶ Prepare the parent sheet and the pieces to be fused onto it with flux and place in position.

❷ Apply heat initially to the underside and, as the silver starts to become red, bring the flame round to the top. As the heat increases, the silver pieces start to melt and the parent sheet will look shiny. At this point, drag the "shiny" look down the piece with the flame, making sure the shininess is visible around the bottom of each piece.

❸ Turn off the heat and allow the piece to air-cool for a minute or so before quenching and pickling to ensure it is perfectly clean.

The surface of the silver becomes liquid as fusing takes place.

WORKING THE PIECE

❶ If small, flat pieces of contrasting metal have been fused to a silver sheet, put it through the rolling mill to flatten the pieces into the metal, or roll with some emery paper, to achieve a beautiful effect.

❷ The fused piece is now ready to be worked. If any small fused pieces lift away during fabrication, anneal the pieces and push them back down again, and then re-fuse. If any soldering has taken place before the fused piece lifts away, then anneal the whole piece, push the fused piece back down into position, flux it, and place tiny pieces of solder at the edges, so that it can be soldered back into position.

Very finely ground gold was fused onto a piece of silver and passed through a rolling mill.

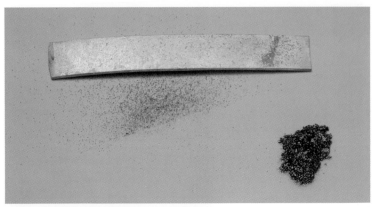

For an interesting undulating effect, direct a very hot flame onto the edge of silver.

SAMPLES • **Fusing**

For a really interesting surface texture, try fusing the metal—either by heating it alone to a stage just before it starts to melt, or by adding small pieces of the same or contrasting metals. Fusing can be used to create complete pieces, for example, in joining a silver or high-carat gold ring, without the need to solder.

HOW THE SAMPLES WERE ACHIEVED

SUBSTRATE 1-8

SILVER

❶ Small pieces of silver from a scrap box were fluxed and placed onto a background sheet. Enough heat was applied to fuse them all together.

❷ Different lengths of silver were placed onto a background sheet thin enough just to begin to melt when fused, and to form a hole where desired.

❸ Copper wire was fused onto a silver background by heating the silver surface until it began to shine, the point at which it takes hold of the copper wire.

❹ Filings were made from scrap silver using a coarse flat file. The surface of the background sheet was fluxed, and the filings were scattered on and fused.

❺ Shapes were pierced out of 0.5mm sheet silver, then fluxed and placed on a 1mm-thick background sheet and heated until the metals fused.

❻ Flux was mixed with gum tragacanth to form a paste which was painted in random circles onto a silver sheet. Gold filings were scattered over the gummed areas. The surface was heated until it started to melt and take hold of the gold.

❼ 0.1mm 24-carat gold strips were cut, fluxed, and fused in their centers to form the crosses. The crosses were placed on a fluxed silver surface and fused to it.

❽ Six different-size holes were drilled into a silver sheet. The sheet was heated until the sides started to move inward, toward the holes.

HELPFUL HINTS

- When using scrap silver for fusing, make sure that any solder is cut out first.
- Fused metal is more brittle than ordinary sheet metal. Do any further work, such as bending or twisting, slowly and carefully, and anneal when necessary.
- A fused piece will take longer to pickle clean. When it is clean, finish with liquid soap and a brass brush.
- Ensure that pieces to be fused are in contact with each other. If they are not touching, they will not fuse but simply melt.
- When fusing a very thin piece of metal to a thicker piece, make sure the thicker piece is very hot before bringing the heat onto the thinner piece.

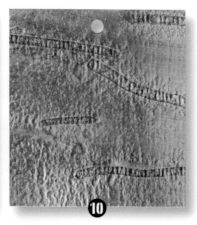

SUBSTRATE 9-12

SILVER

9 The flower was cut from fine silver (which does not oxidize) and hammered into the center, then fluxed and fused onto a standard background. The piece was oxidized, leaving the background dark and the flower pattern unoxidized.

10 Slivers of 24-carat gold were fluxed and fused onto silver, and put through a rolling mill along with a textured fabric.

11 The crater-like appearance was achieved by fusing thin silver pieces onto brass. The heat needed to start to melt the brass also melted the silver.

12 Thick silver was heated until the sides gravitated toward the middle, giving a lunar appearance.

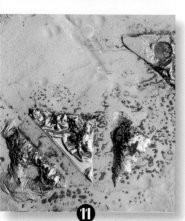

SUBSTRATE 13

GOLD

13 Different thicknesses of 18-carat gold were fused to form an undulating background.

SUBSTRATE 14

BRASS

14 Hammered copper wire was placed onto a fluxed brass sheet and heated until the two metals fused. The resultant hole was trimmed with a piercing saw to enhance the design.

SHOWCASE • **Fusing**

A multitude of effects may be achieved with fusing. The brooches, cufflinks, dotted earrings, and double spiral ring in this showcase demonstrate how precise the technique may be, while the patterned bangles and tiger moth earrings display a less defined look. The fusing of contrasting metals, as seen in all these pieces, always looks wonderful.

PATTERNED BANGLES
Jean Scott-Moncrieff • Sterling silver and 18-carat gold
Fusing has been used on a large surface area for dramatic effect. The curved, polished inner surface of the bangles gives a contrast to the subtle pattern on the flat face.

DOTTED EARRINGS

Chris Carpenter •
22-carat yellow gold,
18-carat white gold,
and sapphires
The dots have been cut, like fat salami slices, from a round wire and fused onto the gold sheet, creating an effective pattern of white on yellow gold.

DOUBLE SPIRAL
Shelby Fitzpatrick • Sterling silver and 22-carat gold
A bold spiral of yellow gold has been fused onto silver for this double ring.

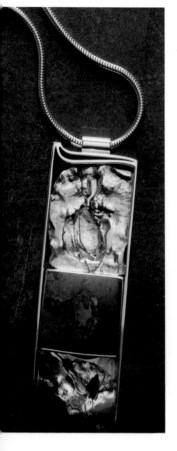

GOLD AND OPAL PENDANT
Jon and Valerie Hill •
18-carat gold and
Australian opal
A beautiful opal and fused gold pieces have been set within a gold frame.

TIGER MOTH EARRINGS
Margaret Shepherd • Sterling silver,
22-carat gold, and cabochon garnets
Tudor Braid pendants set with garnets have been suspended from silver tiger moths with fused gold detail on their upper wings.

PAIR OF BROOCHES
Chris Carpenter • Sterling silver, 22- and 18-carat gold
White gold lines have been fused onto a silver sheet before assembly to make this pair of stylish abstract brooches.

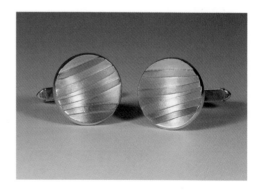

ROUND CUFFLINKS
Robert Feather • 18-carat yellow gold
with white, red, and green gold
Four colors of gold have been fused to yellow gold discs for these cufflinks.

DIRECTORY OF EFFECTS AND TECHNIQUES

TECHNIQUE • **Polished, matt, and satin finishes**

The quality of finishing can turn an ordinary piece of jewelry into something special. Some of the most beautiful pieces of jewelry are very simple, finely crafted silver shapes that have been given a subtle polish or satin finish.

Finishing takes time, but if each step is carefully followed, the results will be well worth the effort. Think about the finished look you desire before starting to make an item. For example, if the hammered finish appeals, work out at what stage of fabrication the metal is to be hammered. This may sound obvious, but it is easy to get underway, only to realize the hammering has become almost impossible to do. All the following finishes can also be achieved by hand, although the polishing machine does speed things up considerably.

POLISHING EQUIPMENT

① *Glass fiber sticks*
② *Fine polishing cloth*
③ *Calico and lambswool mops*
④ *Green polish*
⑤ *Red polish*

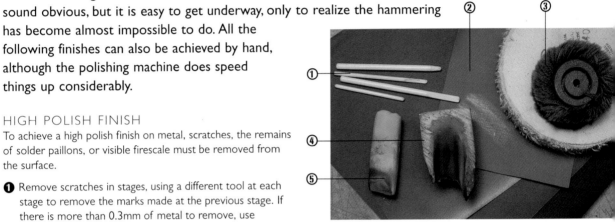

HIGH POLISH FINISH

To achieve a high polish finish on metal, scratches, the remains of solder paillons, or visible firescale must be removed from the surface.

❶ Remove scratches in stages, using a different tool at each stage to remove the marks made at the previous stage. If there is more than 0.3mm of metal to remove, use a fairly coarse file. Once the level is down to 0.1mm, use a a finer needle file. After the needle file, smooth the surface with a progression of grades (from 220 through to 1200) of wet-and-dry papers. Clean any awkward areas by wrapping small pieces of wet-and-dry paper around different-shaped needle files. Use small glass fiber sticks to clean any small and difficult areas.

❷ Polishes and mops are similar to wet-and-dry papers in that there is a specific order in which they should be used. If the work has been finished with paper first, green polish, applied with a calico mop, will be sufficient. If, however, there are some scratches on the surface, it will be necessary to use "Tripoli," a dark, brown-red polish, with a firm, small, calico mop, followed by an application of "Hyfin," a white block polish, with a fresh calico mop. Between each polishing, clean the piece of all traces of polish, either in an ultrasonic cleaner or by hand using a soft brush and liquid soap. Use a lambswool mop and a "rouge" polish for a final polish. Dip the rouge polish in a little kerosene first to prevent it clogging on the metal.

MATT FINISH

To achieve a matt finish, first texture the surface of a piece. This can be a very light texture, as, for example, is obtained by passing the metal through a rolling mill with some cotton wool or paper. Do not touch the surface with a file or paper after the texture has been imprinted and allow the "white" surface to build up with subsequent soldering and pickling. Clean the surface with a pumice paste or fine steel wool and liquid soap to give a clean, matt finish.

Use a burnisher to achieve highlights on the edge of a reticulated piece of silver.

SAFETY

Observe the following rules when using a polishing motor:

● Tie back long hair and avoid wearing long or floppy sleeves and jewelry.
● Hold the item being polished in both hands, just below the horizontal diameter of the polishing mop.
● The motor turns the spindle very fast. Always stay focused on your work.

SATIN FINISH

To achieve a good satin finish, follow the high polish finish procedure and then take the surface back to a matt finish (see previous page). There is less likelihood of visible scratches or firescale if the piece is correctly polished first. It is also possible to achieve a satin finish without high polishing, by using wet-and-dry papers in ascending order. Fine steel wool used with liquid soap on metal will also give a smooth satin finish, as will fine pumice powder mixed to a paste and rubbed on with the fingers. A fine stainless steel mop on the polishing machine will give a steel-satin finish.

REMOVING FIRESCALE

When high-polishing silver, grayish shadows may appear on the surface. This is known as firescale and is the copper content in standard silver revealed after the silver has been heated. It can be a real nuisance and is difficult to remove.

USING FLUX

It is possible to prevent firescale when making a piece from silver, although this is only practical if the item is fairly large. To do so, before heating the silver, paint the entire surface with either flux or an anti-firescale paste to prevent air getting at the surface and causing oxidization.

When soldering, keep the flux or anti-firescale paste at least $^1/_4$ to $^1/_2$ inch/5 to 10mm away from the solder line. Flux the solder line as normal to allow the solder to flow. If the two areas of flux do meet, the solder tends to run into the pasted area and not into the join. After soldering, pickle the piece and remove the flux or paste. Any subsequent heating will require a fresh coat. This process is too time-consuming to be useful on small items.

Pumice powder used with a damp toothbrush is an excellent metal cleaner and leaves an interesting "gray" finish on silver. Steel wool used with a liquid soap brightens the surface. Stainless steel mops can be used to give a coarse, medium, or fine texture on the metal.

POLISHING

❶ If the piece is made from sufficiently thick metal, remove firescale by polishing. This entails polishing harder than would otherwise be necessary, with consequently more silver loss. However, if slightly heavier or thicker metal is used, the loss through polishing will be sustainable.

❷ Before polishing, remove as much visible gray as possible with a needle file. Providing the piece is not heated up again, it will remain scale-free.

❸ After polishing, if there are still areas of gray scale, use a Water of Ayr stone. This is a fine stone which, when dipped in water and rubbed on the surface of metal, will gradually remove the scale. Work it into a thick paste and, once the firescale is removed, polish the piece immediately, without filing or using wet-and-dry papers.

ANNEALING AND PICKLING

Working silver by annealing, soldering, and pickling several times builds up a white coating of fine silver, which does not oxidize with repeated heating. The more the silver is annealed and pickled, the thicker the layer becomes, because each time it is pickled, the copper content on the surface is removed. If you can leave the piece in this condition, there will be no visible firescale. If you can keep subsequent work to a minimum, with no hard polishing, this fine silver will prevent the appearance of gray areas.

SILVER PLATING

When a piece is finished, have it professionally plated to deposit a layer of fine silver over the whole piece to cover, but not remove, any firescale.

Remove firescale that appears on silver after it has been polished with a Water of Ayr stone. Dampen the stone in water and rub hard over the affected area.

SAMPLES • **Polished, matt, and satin finishes**

The finish on a piece can make or break it. These samples show a variety of finishes. Try combining different treatments for an unusual effect: give the background of a piece a matt finish and the central decoration a polished finish, or polish the edges of a satin-finished piece with a burnisher for a framed effect. A good finish takes time, but is worth it.

DIRECTORY OF EFFECTS AND TECHNIQUES

HOW THE SAMPLES WERE ACHIEVED

SUBSTRATE 1-4

SILVER

❶ Matt finish achieved using 220-grade wet-and-dry paper on the surface, followed by the gentle application of a stainless steel burnisher to give the mottled effect.

❷ Matt finish achieved by progressively working through grades 220 to 600 wet-and-dry papers, then applying a moistened, soap-filled, steel wool pad to the surface.

❸ Following the application of a progression of 220 to 600 wet-and-dry papers the surface was rubbed with a glass brush, used with running water, with liquid soap.

❹ Following the progression of wet-and-dry papers, as in sample 3, a brass brush was loaded with liquid soap and rubbed vigorously over the surface. (Liquid soap must be used with a brass brush to avoid a fine layer of brass being deposited on the surface).

SUBSTRATE 5-6

COPPER

❺ The copper was first finished with a progression of wet-and-dry papers from 220 to 1200, and then polished with a calico mop and green (general purpose) polish on the polishing machine.

❻ "Dull" finish achieved using a progression of wet-and-dry papers from grades 220 to 600, and then polished on a machine with a bristle mop and "Tripoli" polish. A finer finish can be achieved by following with a polish of "Hyfin."

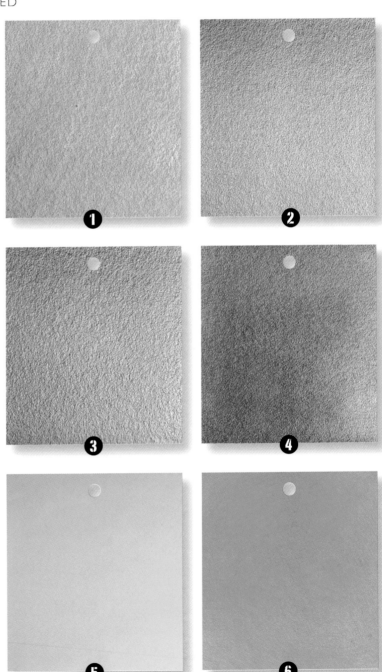

HELPFUL HINTS

- Before starting to polish, or to give a piece its finish, make sure there are no file marks or obvious scratches left on the metal.
- After polishing, remove any excess polish either by boiling the piece in water with a little ammonia and liquid soap, or by using an ultrasonic cleaner. Do not rub it with anything that might scratch it again, such as paper or a coarse cloth.
- Always use grades of wet-and-dry papers in numerical ascending order: 220 is coarse and 1200 is fine.
- A finish is generally the last thing to be done on a piece. However, if any more soldering is required after polishing, anneal and pickle the piece first and wipe with some acetone to make sure that all the polish grease has been removed. The piece can then be soldered.

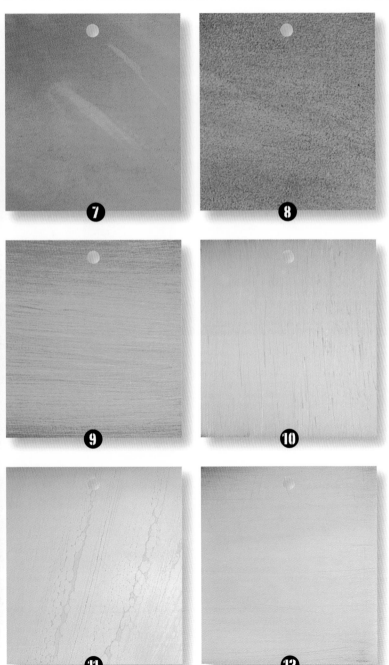

SUBSTRATE 7-8

COPPER

7 After the progression of wet-and-dry papers, as before, green polish was applied with a calico mop. The finish was achieved using the polishing machine and a fine stainless steel mop.

8 The crystalline appearance was achieved by first following the method in sample 7, but using a coarse stainless steel mop on the polishing machine.

SUBSTRATE 9-12

BRASS

9 Satin finish achieved by rubbing 220-grade wet-and-dry paper evenly (with or without water) over the surface.

10 Finer satin finish made by first rubbing evenly with 220-grade wet-and-dry paper and then rubbing crosswise with 400-grade wet-and-dry paper. Finally, 600-grade wet-and-dry paper was rubbed in the same direction as the 220-grade.

11 Finish achieved by first following the method in sample 10. A final polish was applied using "Crocus" paper, a very fine, dark red paper used in the same way as other abrasive papers, but dry.

12 Satin finish achieved as in sample 10, with the further, final addition of a liquid brass or silver polish. The metal was vigorously rubbed over a rag soaked in a liquid polish, laid on a flat surface.

SHOWCASE • **Polished, matt, and satin finishes**

All these pieces were made using a range of techniques and surface decoration. But what a difference the finish makes! From the soft satin gleam of the long drop earrings to the high polish of the *Cofio II* ring and bangle, each piece is a wonderful example of the way a different finish can alter the feeling of a work.

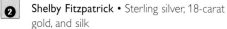
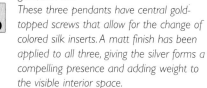

SCREW-TOP PENDANTS

Shelby Fitzpatrick • Sterling silver, 18-carat gold, and silk

These three pendants have central gold-topped screws that allow for the change of colored silk inserts. A matt finish has been applied to all three, giving the silver forms a compelling presence and adding weight to the visible interior space.

COFIO/REMEMBER II

Mari Thomas • Sterling silver

In this ring and bangle set, the fluid motif and high polish on the outer surface of the pieces contrasts with the etched text and frosted finish which has been applied to the interior.

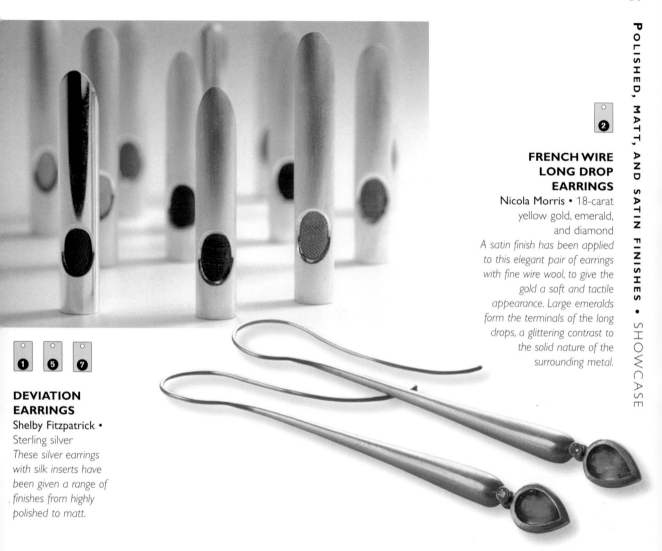

FRENCH WIRE LONG DROP EARRINGS

Nicola Morris • 18-carat yellow gold, emerald, and diamond

A satin finish has been applied to this elegant pair of earrings with fine wire wool, to give the gold a soft and tactile appearance. Large emeralds form the terminals of the long drops, a glittering contrast to the solid nature of the surrounding metal.

DEVIATION EARRINGS

Shelby Fitzpatrick • Sterling silver

These silver earrings with silk inserts have been given a range of finishes from highly polished to matt.

THREE CURVES NECKLACE

Jinks McGrath • Silver, 18-carat gold, and labradorite

The shape of the labradorite stone, set into 18-carat gold, is echoed by the three pieces of silver and 18-carat gold that curve gently around it. The necklace exudes tranquility; the soft matt finish is the perfect enhancement.

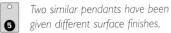

DOUGHNUT PENDANTS

Shelby Fitzpatrick • Sterling silver and silk

Two similar pendants have been given different surface finishes, highlighting the importance that simple visual information can have on a piece as a whole. The way in which polish creates indeterminate reflected patterns can be clearly seen on the left-hand form.

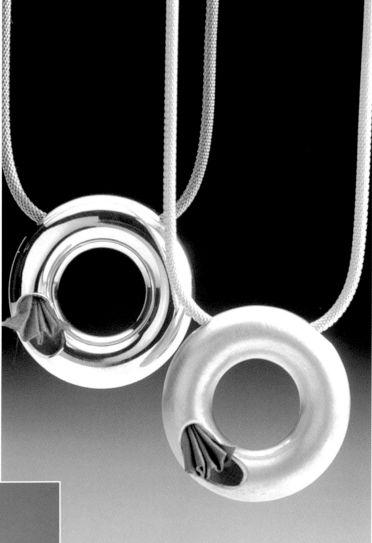

BAGUE SVÉTA

Antoine Chapoutot • 18-carat yellow gold and Tahiti pearl

The brushed gold section of this gorgeous ring snugly holds a pearl against the highly-polished shank. The reflections created in the recess invite the viewer to explore the piece more thoroughly.

EGG-LINK BANGLE
Nicola Morris • Sterling silver

For this cast-silver bangle, the designer has used a high-rouge polish to give a sense of ambiguity to the form. High polish can bring an almost liquid quality to the surface of a metal.

WHITE AND YELLOW GOLD NECKLACE
Jinks McGrath • 18-carat yellow and white gold with diamond

The simple pendant on this necklace displays both matt and polished areas. The central white gold disc is shiny, attracting the eye to the center of the form where a single diamond is cradled. The slightly textured yellow gold disc surrounding the diamond gives the piece volume, creating contrast in both color and surface finish.

TECHNIQUE • Etching

The etching process offers many possibilities for creating different patterns and free-form designs. It provides an opportunity to achieve interesting finishes on metal and to allow your imagination to run wild!

During the etching process, a chosen area of the metal is removed by being placed into an acid solution, known as "mordant." The acid eats away at the metal until it is removed and rinsed under running water. Areas of metal that are not to be etched are covered with a "stop-out" in the form of either a varnish, a black bitumen-based liquid, beeswax, or a hard or soft ground stop-out, which is a mixture of beeswax, bitumen, and rosin.

ETCHING MATERIALS
① *Container with water*
② *Stop-out fluid*
③ *4:1 water-nitric acid solution*
④ *Scalpel*
⑤ *Assorted brushes*

When a decorative surface is required, the etch needs to be just deep enough to provide a distinct difference between the levels. However, if the area to be etched is for champlevé enameling (see page 95), the depth of etch should reach between 0.3mm and 0.5mm. Care should be taken to ensure the acid does not "undercut" the edges which would spoil the definition of the enamel.

SOLUTIONS, OR MORDANTS

Different mordants are used for etching different metals. The more commonly used ones are listed below with recommendations for the type of container.

GOLD: 40 parts water to four parts Aqua Regia (one part nitric acid to three parts hydrochloric acid)—in a glass container.

SILVER, COPPER, AND BRASS: three or four parts water to one part nitric acid—in a glass container.

ENAMEL: 10 parts water to one or two parts hydrofluoric acid—in a plastic container.

SAFETY

When mixing mordants, the following safety measures should be observed:

● Add acid to water—never water to acid. If the mixture is too strong, add the mixture to the required amount of water, don't pour the water into the mixture.
● Wear rubber gloves and eye protection when handling acid.
● Mix mordants in an area that is well ventilated.
● Use plastic tweezers to handle work in mordant.
● Store mordants in a glass or plastic container with a tightly-fitting cap or screw-top. When not in use, the container should be kept in a locked cupboard.
● The piece should be thoroughly rinsed in water after removal from the mordant.

PREPARING THE METAL

❶ If a precise pattern is being etched onto the metal, as, for example, when enameling, the areas which are to be removed are outlined with a scribe (see Transferring a Pattern to a Metal, page 103). Work with a sheet of metal larger than the pattern required. The acid sometimes eats into the edges of the work, despite the stop-out, and if there is extra metal around the pattern, this can be pierced away later.

❷ Anneal, pickle, and rinse the metal.

❸ Clean the metal under running water with a glass brush, soft brass brush, or very fine wet-and-dry paper, until the water spreads over the whole piece and does not form small globules. Make sure that all the edges and corners are clean, then dry it and place it on a small rack.

❹ The lines made with the scribe will now be visible on the metal. Paint stop-out fluid onto the whole surface up to the scribed lines and along all the edges. When this is dry, which may take between 30 to 60 minutes depending on how thickly the stop-out is applied, turn the piece over and paint the reverse with stop-out. Allow this to dry.

❺ If the desired look is more like a sketch, then the etch is less defined, and the front, back, and sides of the metal should be painted with stop-out. After it has thoroughly dried, the lines of the pattern are sketched or scraped through the stop-out with a scribe, or other sharp tool.

Reinforce the penciled line of the pattern by going over it with a sharp scribe.

To paint on stop-out, lay the piece across two supports. Paint the sides of the metal at the same time as the top. Let dry completely before turning it over and painting the back.

When the stop-out has dried, a scribe is used to scratch through it to sketch the design.

ETCHING THE METAL

1 Now immerse the piece in the mordant. The length of time required for each etch varies. Use a goose feather every 10 minutes or so to gently brush the top of the piece, to clear away the etched metal and to keep the solution slightly agitated. If the solution is warm, or the proportions altered so that the ratio of the acid is higher, the etch will occur faster. Etching too quickly is not recommended as this will undercut the lines more easily.

2 When the required depth of etch has been reached, remove the metal from the mordant and rinse well in water. Remove the stop-out with white spirit, denatured alcohol, or kerosene and clean well with soap and a soft brush.

3 Pierce the outside line to achieve the final shape.

Apply stop-out with a sponge for a random etch. Paint the sides and back completely.

PHOTOETCHING

Photoetching is a process that photosensitizes the metal, to act as a resist in some areas and print the image on the rest. The piece is then immersed in a suitable mordant to be etched.

Photoetching requires a lot of space and tanks of acid and is therefore not usually done at home. You will need to send your artwork to a commercial photoetching firm.

Photoetching is difficult to achieve on a small scale as the sheets of metal used must be at least 18 x 12 inches/45 x 30cm. It is, however, a very practical way of repeating a pattern and achieving a very accurate edge. An etch of different depths, for example, 0.3mm and 0.6mm, can be achieved on the same sheet. It will also cut right through the metal, to a depth of $1/16$ inch/1.2mm.

Prepare the artwork for photoetching by drawing and painting an accurate image of the patterns at twice the size of the finished piece. Reduce this by half using a copier to give an even greater accuracy. Paint the areas that are to be etched as a solid color; this is what produces the image on the metal sheet.

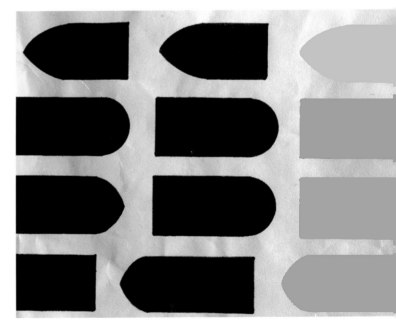

Paint your designs at twice the desired size and then use a copier to reduce the artwork by half before sending to a professional photoetching firm.

The photoetching firm will send your photoetched patterns back in large sheets that must be cut up. Use a pair of dividers to mark a fine line at an exact and equal distance around the pattern you require before piercing the piece from the rest of the sheet.

Use a pair of dividers opened out to the width of the edge to be pierced, and run one side up the inside edge of the cut-away area, so that the other side can mark the metal with a fine line.

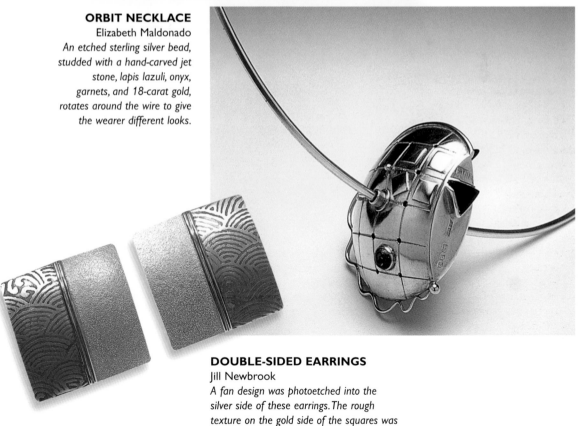

ORBIT NECKLACE
Elizabeth Maldonado
An etched sterling silver bead, studded with a hand-carved jet stone, lapis lazuli, onyx, garnets, and 18-carat gold, rotates around the wire to give the wearer different looks.

DOUBLE-SIDED EARRINGS
Jill Newbrook
A fan design was photoetched into the silver side of these earrings. The rough texture on the gold side of the squares was achieved by passing the metal through the rolling mill with some emery paper.

SAMPLES • **Etching**

Use etching to create either a very exact pattern, or something more random and sketchy. The depth of etch is entirely up to you—a depth of approximately 0.1mm will show up well on a metal surface, while the depth of etch for enameling should be at least 0.3mm. Once a surface has been etched, try using other techniques, such as oxidizing and or adding gold leaf, to enhance and emphasize the effect.

HOW THE SAMPLES WERE ACHIEVED

SUBSTRATE 1–7

COPPER ETCHED IN NITRIC ACID

❶ Effect achieved by randomly painting the front and back in stop-out fluid.

❷ The back and front were completely covered with stop-out fluid, and the scene scratched through dried stop-out fluid with a sharp steel point.

❸ The metal was first heated, then quenched. The back and sides were covered with stop-out fluid, and a sponge used to daub stop-out fluid on the front.

❹ Effect achieved by dropping heated beeswax onto front and completely covering the back with stop-out fluid.

❺ Effect achieved by painting stop-out fluid on the back, edges and in random circles, allowing the background and inside the circles to be etched.

❻ Open-weave fabric was glued onto the metal and the fabric, back and sides were painted with stop-out fluid. When dry, the fabric was removed before the metal was etched.

❼ Effect achieved by etching twice: first, stop-out fluid was painted up to outside pattern line and the whole interior area etched to a depth of 0.3mm. Stop-out fluid was then applied to both inside and outside areas, leaving only the thick line to be etched.

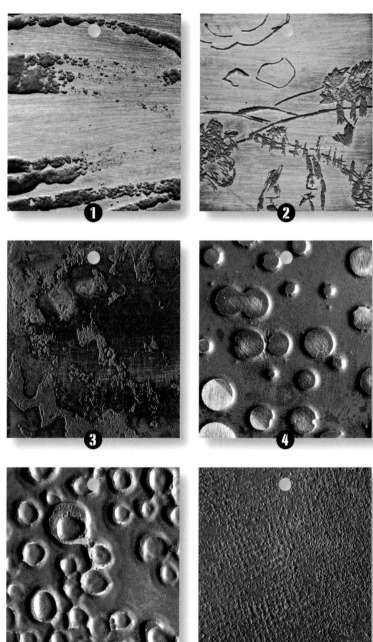

HELPFUL HINTS

- When working with acids, work in a well ventilated area and wear a mask and rubber gloves.
- Before painting on the stop-out fluid or applying wax, make sure the metal is clean and free from grease.
- Heat with a soldering torch to remove stop-out or wax.
- Silver will fizz if the mordant is too strong. However, copper will always fizz in a nitric acid-water mordant.

- DO NOT add water to acid; ONLY add acid to water.
- If the stop-out fluid starts to lift off when the piece is in the mordant, carefully remove the piece with a pair of plastic or stainless-steel tweezers, rinse it under running cold water, and dry it with some absorbent paper. When it is completely dry, repaint the area that has lifted. Allow it to dry before replacing the piece in the mordant.

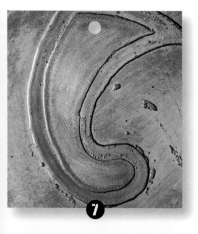

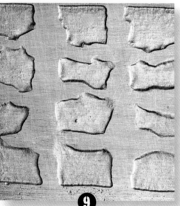
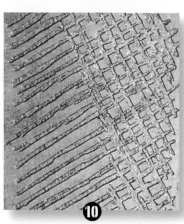

SUBSTRATE 8

SILVER

8 This pattern was etched for enameling. The shape was scribed onto silver and the rest of the piece covered with stop-out fluid. It was etched to a depth of 0.3mm, deep enough for cloisonné wire to be used for enameling.

SUBSTRATE 9-10

BRASS

9 Effect achieved by dropping melted beeswax in a criss-cross pattern.
10 Effect achieved by covering the piece with stop-out fluid, and when dry, using a sharp steel point to make the cross-hatching pattern before etching.

SUBSTRATE 11-12

SILVER

11 A pattern was first drawn on paper before being sent to be photoetched into the metal.
12 The pattern was also drawn on paper before the metal was photoetched.

SHOWCASE • **Etching**

The versatility offered by the etching technique is seen in this showcase.
Some of the pieces use etching as a means of showing a contrasting color,
such as a colored lacquer, the black of oxidization, or the yellow of gold inlay.
In others, the etching is left plain to display the texture and height contrasts
left on the surface by the etch.

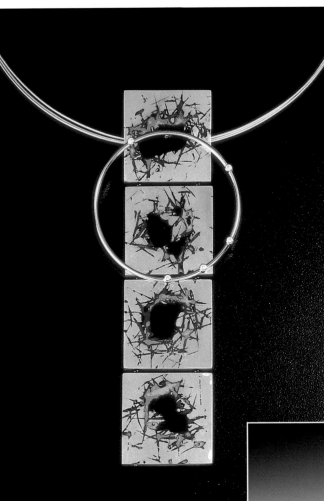

DAYBREAK II
Kuo-Jen Chen • Sterling silver,
diamond, lacquer, and 18-carat gold
*Lacquer has been introduced into
the etched recesses of this
expressive neckpiece.*

HOLLOW SHAPES
COLLECTION
Elizabeth Maldonaldo • Sterling silver,
18-carat gold, and tourmalines
*The etched detail appears both on
the inside and outside of the shapes of
this collection comprising a brooch,
pendant, and three rings. Gold motifs
have been used to enhance features
of the geometric designs.*

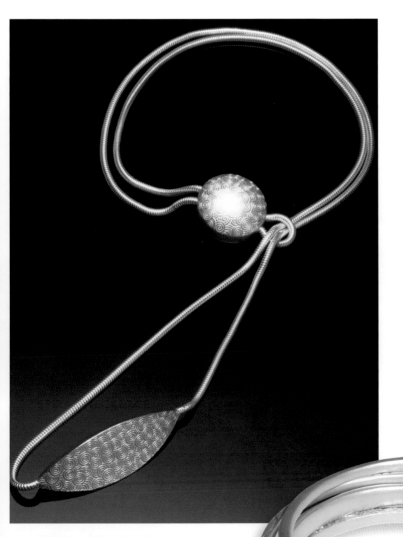

GEOMETRIC EARRINGS
Lisbeth Dauv • Sterling silver
with 24-carat gold
*A geometric pattern has been
etched onto the surface of
these earrings and a gold
spiral has been applied for
decorative effect.*

⑤

BANGLE STACK
Diana Porter • Sterling silver
and 22-carat yellow gold
*Etching is a very effective way
of introducing text on to metal,
as can be seen in these
lustrous bangles.*

⑩

SPIRAL NECKLACE
Shelby Fitzpatrick • Sterling silver
*Photoetching has been used on the
hollow forms of this necklace to
create a striking spiral pattern.*

⑪

"AND ON" COLLECTION
Diana Porter • Silver and 22-carat yellow-gold
etch, using acid with sandblast finish
*22-carat gold has been applied to the areas that
have been etched away to create a glowing recess of
words. A sandblasted finish has been used.*

⑩

10

JAPAN EARRINGS/BROOCHES
Elizabeth Maldonaldo • Sterling silver and 18-carat gold
The spinal structure of these pieces allows them to be worn as either earrings or brooches. The form has been embellished with etching, oxidizing, and gold rivets.

11

PATTERNED BRACELET
Jill Newbrook • Sterling silver
and 22-carat gold
*Such accuracy of pattern can only
be achieved with photoetching, the
effect of which has been enhanced
here with oxidization.*

8

GWYNT YR HWYR/ THE EVENING BREEZE
Mari Thomas • Sterling silver
*Etching has been used
to create raised text on
these pieces as well as
an abstract pattern.*

PENDANTS

Shelby Fitzpatrick • Sterling silver
*For these two pendants, the designer has
oxidized the photoetched recess on one, and
used gold plate for the other. The pendants
can also be worn as rings.*

DRIFT STARS BROOCH

Kuo-Jen Chen • 18-carat gold
*This gold brooch has been etched
and lacquered to produce these
beautiful colors.*

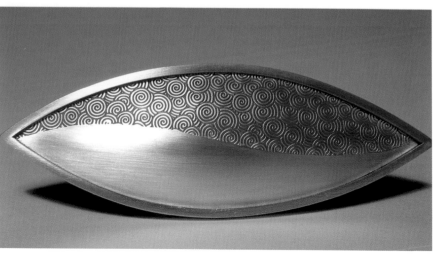

SPIRALS BROOCH

Jill Newbrook • Sterling silver
*The etched pattern on this
brooch almost gives it an extra
dimension as the tiny spirals
divert the eye across its surface.*

TECHNIQUE • Patination and oxidization

Patina is defined as "any thin film, coloring, or mellowed appearance on the surface of an object as a result of age or use." On copper and bronze, a patina tends to be either green or blue, and on silver a dark gray color. This coloration is due to exposure to air and the effect that various particles have upon the surface. As the natural process can take some time, there are ways to achieve the "aged" appearance and color by using chemicals on different metals.

PATINATION MATERIALS
① *Lumps of potassium sulfide*
② *Airtight container with mixture of sawdust and ammonia*

When metal is heated, wonderful colors occur through oxidization. These colors are not always stable, especially if the piece requires further work, or if it needs pickling which removes all traces of flux and oxidization. Occasionally, despite both soldering and pickling, the colors that appear as a result of heating copper will remain

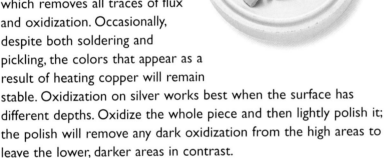

stable. Oxidization on silver works best when the surface has different depths. Oxidize the whole piece and then lightly polish it; the polish will remove any dark oxidization from the high areas to leave the lower, darker areas in contrast.

Consider whether to patinate or oxidize before starting work on a piece. Most colors will disappear when a piece is soldered and subsequently pickled, so create any coloring once the working is completed. If, however, sheet metal is only being pierced and drilled, then patination can be done at the start of the work.

When trying out patination, do not be afraid to experiment. The recipes here are dependent on time, the cleanliness of the metal, whether the metal has been annealed or not, or exposed to the air. When you find the mixture that you like, write it down so that you can repeat it.

SAFETY

- All the mixtures used in patination or oxidization processes have strong fumes, so work must take place in a well-ventilated space with easy access to running water.
- Wear a face mask to prevent inhalation of fumes, and wear rubber gloves when handling any of the mediums, or the metals which have residue of the mixture on them.

PREPARING THE METALS

Metals to be patinated must be totally clean and free of grease, so that water will sit evenly on the surface and not form into globules. To achieve this, the work can be annealed, pickled, and rinsed, or cleaned with a pumice paste, or with a glass brush. Any signs of excess solder must be filed and cleaned away.

PATINATING COPPER

The following process produces a deep red-purple finish:

❶ Take a sheet of copper, 3¹/₄ x 2 x ¹/₁₆ inches/8cm x 5cm x 1mm. Clean both sides under running water with wet-and-dry paper to ensure that the surfaces are perfectly clean.

❷ Paint both sides with a flux paste—either borax flux, or a powder flux.

❸ Heat the copper on one side with a strong, hot flame until it glows orange. Turn it over and heat the other side to the same color. Then quench it in water and pickle for a few minutes.

❹ The copper should be a beautiful red-purple color. If not, repeat the process. Gently polish or lightly oil the copper with either jade oil or soft beeswax.

The following process produces a green-blue color:

❶ Fill a sealable plastic container with sawdust or rolling tobacco.

❷ Measure one part vinegar and three parts household ammonia into a glass measuring jug. Pour enough of this solution into the container to dampen the sawdust.

❸ Clean the copper by annealing and pickling and then rubbing with wet-and-dry paper under running water. The water should stay evenly all over the surface. Let dry.

❹ Place the copper in the sawdust and cover it completely. Seal the container. Allow it to stand for at least one hour, but preferably up to two days.

❺ The copper can be removed when the desired degree of green has appeared. The plastic container and tobacco can be stored for future use.

The plastic container has a tightly fitting lid so that the smell of the fumes does not drift out into the workshop. The copper piece was left in the sawdust for a couple of days.

The following process produces blue:

❶ Fill an open container, such as a small saucer or inverted jar top, with some household ammonia.

❷ Cover the copper with some salt.

❸ Dampen the salt with water or vinegar.

❹ Place both the copper and the container with ammonia in an airtight space, either by covering them with a plastic container or by placing them in a plastic container with a sealable lid.

❺ Allow the copper to stand for at least a few hours, but preferably up to two days. The copper can be removed when coloration is complete. Replace the ammonia in its original container.

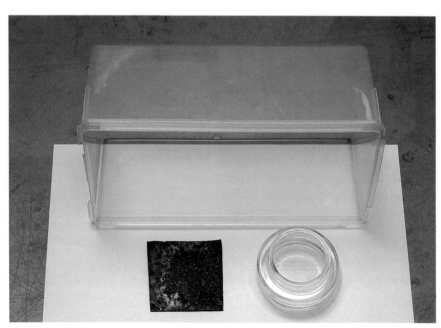

Salt was placed on the copper piece, ammonia poured carefully into the small glass container, and the plastic container set over both.

OXIDIZING SILVER

Oxidize silver once all soldering and filing is completed. If, having oxidized a piece of silver, you do not like the color, it can be annealed and pickled again to remove the coloration.

Potassium sulfide in lump form is required for the process. It should be stored in an airtight container and kept in a cool, dark place. If allowed to deteriorate it will not produce the colors required.

During the oxidizing process, the silver passes through several different color stages from yellow through pink, to blue-purple to black. To hold any of these colors, the piece can be removed very quickly from the dip and neutralized in water.

The following process produces a deep black color:

❶ Find an area on the work from which a little silver hook can be hung so that the piece can be suspended in liquid. If this is not possible, the work can be placed in the liquid using plastic tweezers.

❷ Place about a teaspoon of potassium sulfide in a measuring jug. Cover with boiling water. Allow to dissolve.

❸ Stir the liquid with a wooden or plastic stirrer and immediately hang the silver piece into the liquid. Keep the silver immersed until it is a deep black color.

❹ Remove the silver from the liquid and rinse it thoroughly under the cold tap.

Potassium sulfide in little lumps. Dissolve a few lumps in very hot water and use the solution fairly quickly.

Suspend the piece being oxidized in the solution until the desired color is reached and then rinse in clear water.

COPPER JEWELRY BOX
Penny Warren
The side panel of this copper box was patinated red before being lightly repousséd with a random flower pattern. Wet-and-dry papers were then gently rubbed over the panel to reveal the original copper color on the high points of the punching.

The following process produces a range of colors:

The color from this method is not very durable, so it is best for areas of a silver piece which will get less wear. It is very effective in deepened areas.

1 Clean the silver to be colored and make sure it is free from any polish or grease. Hang the silver from a hook made from silver or strong thread.

2 Prepare everything first, as the coloring occurs at different stages of dipping. Stand a pan of hot water on a low heat to keep it hot. Prepare a potassium sulfide solution (see the previous page) and keep warm if possible. Prepare two cold water rinses.

3 Place the hook onto the silver piece and hang it in the pan of hot water long enough for it to become hot. Then hang it in the potassium sulfide solution and watch carefully for the color you desire to appear. Immediately it reaches that color, lift it out and plunge it into the first cold water rinse. Follow quickly with the second cold water rinse.

4 Rinse again under a cold faucet and remove any unwanted color with a gentle polish.

These silver necklace pieces were first heated in hot water and then held for different lengths of time in the potassium sulfide solution. The lengths of time ranged from 3 seconds for the piece colored silvery-gold to 1 minute for the black piece.

HEAT-OXIDIZED MESH NECKPIECES
Reinier Brom
Steel, copper, and brass has been oxidized to produce the antiqued coloration on these three neckpieces. The suggestion of ancient times is echoed in the torc-like shape.

SAMPLES • Patination and oxidization

These samples are just an indication of the range of colors that can be achieved using different chemicals on different metals. Effects from patination and oxidization vary tremendously; if your piece doesn't look exactly the same as the sample, just keep experimenting!

HOW THE SAMPLES WERE ACHIEVED

SUBSTRATE 1-6

COPPER

❶ Both sides were covered with flux. One side was heated until colored very orange, then the work was turned and the other side treated in the same way. The piece was then quenched.

❷ Copper was annealed, put through a rolling mill with soft "grill" mild steel material, placed in a hot potassium sulfide solution, rinsed, and dried. Relief areas were buffed with fine wet-and-dry papers.

❸ Copper, colored by heating and quenching, was passed through a rolling mill with shredded paper, then oxidized lightly in potassium sulfide, rinsed, dried, and the relief points buffed.

❹ Copper was placed in a sealable plastic container with some ammonia, and salt and vinegar sprinkled over the top. It was sealed and allowed to stand for two days.

❺ Copper was coated with flux, heated, quenched, and passed through a rolling mill with string wrapped around it. It was then placed in sunlight and sprayed with a solution of eight parts water, two parts ammonia, and two parts vinegar. This process was repeated four or five times until the color was achieved.

❻ The green color was produced using ammonium chloride with tobacco.

SUBSTRATE 7-8

BRASS

❼ The same effect as in sample 4 is achieved on brass, using the same method, although brass does not always react as easily as copper.

❽ Brass was placed in an airtight plastic container with garden soil, ammonia, and vinegar, and left for three days.

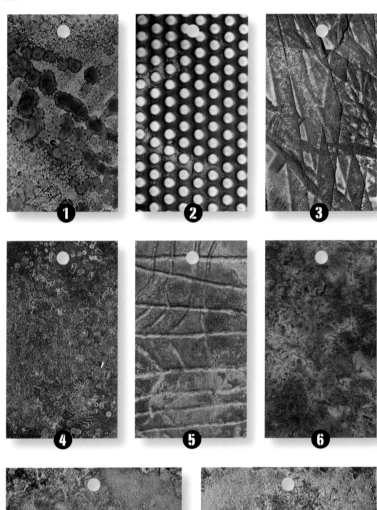

HELPFUL HINTS

- Before patinating or oxidizing, make sure that the metal is free of grease or polish.
- Some colors will take longer to develop than others. Check your piece regularly and remove when the desired color is achieved.
- Work in a well-ventilated area; some of these recipes will produce unpleasant odors.
- Remember that it is easier to oxidize into a recess than onto a flat surface.
- Remove unwanted oxidization by annealing, pickling, and cleaning with liquid soap.

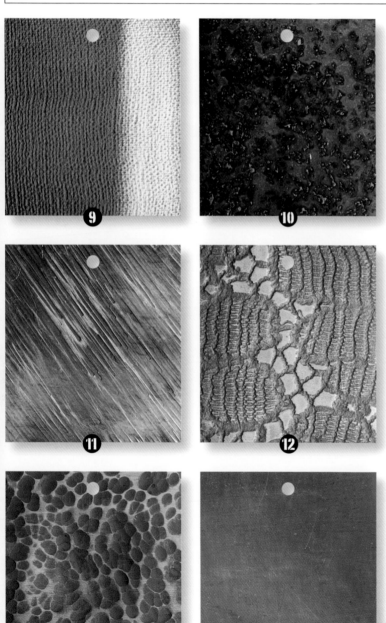

SUBSTRATE 9-10

BRASS

⑨ Placed in a warm potassium sulfide solution and left for 5 to 10 minutes, brass becomes darker. The lighter end of this piece was rubbed with some wet-and-dry paper.

⑩ The mottled effect was produced by submerging brass for two days in a sealable plastic container with rolling tobacco, ammonia, and vinegar.

SUBSTRATE 11-14

SILVER

⑪ After annealing and hammering, silver was dipped quickly into hot potassium sulfide. As soon as colors started to appear, it was put under running cold water.

⑫ Silver was first textured with lace through a rolling mill and placed in a warm pickle of alum with coiled binding wire to deposit copper, producing a pink coloration. The silver was removed and the high areas of the pattern rubbed with wet-and-dry paper to expose the true silver color.

⑬ Silver, hammered with the ball of a ball-pein hammer, was oxidized in hot potassium sulfide. The indentations hold the oxidization and the relief areas can be rubbed clean.

⑭ Effect achieved by placing silver in a hot pickle of one tablespoon of alum dissolved in 1 cup/250ml water. Some iron binding wire was added, which leaves a pink copper deposit on the silver.

SHOWCASE • **Patination and oxidization**

The pieces in this showcase demonstrate some of the variety of finishes offered by the simple process of oxidization. These range from the appearance of aging to some very contemporary effects. Use it to emphasize background or engraved areas, as shown here in the rondelle necklace and the rabbit ring.

13

FIVE BANGLES
Kyoko Urino • Sterling silver
Oxidization has been used on this set of bangles as a means of visually linking the pieces. Each bangle is unique, yet seems to belong on this custom-made display stand.

13

VITIS AMABILIS NECKLACE
Suzan Rezac • Sterling silver and 18-carat gold
The silver structure of this beautifully organic neckpiece has been oxidized black to give greater emphasis to the delicate gold flowers.

RONDELLE NECKLACE
Elizabeth Maldonaldo •
Sterling silver with Chinese
turquoise beads
*Oxidization, left in the recesses
created by the etching process,
emphasizes the design on
the handformed beads,
one of which also
forms a clever
"invisible" clasp.*

WIRE RING
Kyoko Urino • Sterling
silver and gold plate
*The designer has used three
colors of silver wire to make
this textural woven ring.
Gold plating and oxidization
accentuate the depth that
has been created by the
layers of weaving.*

RING COLLECTION
Shimara Carlow • Sterling silver and
18-carat gold
*This set of rings displays the classic
color combinations often used to give
variety to jewelry. The gold ring is offset
by two silver rings, one pickled white,
the other oxidized very black.*

SILVER RABBIT RING
Harriet St Leger • Sterling silver
*This playful ring has been oxidized to
enhance its design. The raised surfaces have
been polished to give a color contrast to the
darker background.*

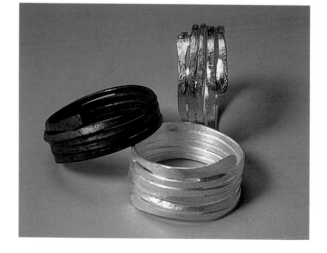

TECHNIQUE • **Casting**

Casting molten metal into a mold can produce stunning effects on a finished surface. There are two simple methods of casting. The first uses the backbone of a cuttlefish to create a pattern or model. The second method makes an impression to receive the molten metal in a special casting sand. A third method, known as lost wax casting, is three-dimensional casting rather than a decorative form. Space does not permit coverage of lost wax casting here—there are several recommended books that deal in detail with this method (see the list of further reading, page 128).

SANDCASTING EQUIPMENT
① Wooden mallet
② Steel ruler
③ Palette knife
④ Drill bits
⑤ Fitted pieces of aluminum tube
⑥ Casting sand

CUTTLEFISH CASTING EQUIPMENT
Cuttlefish

CUTTLEFISH

Cuttlefish can be purchased from jewelry supply shops, pet shops, or found on the waterline of the shore. Those that are fattest through the middle, and preferably without broken edges, are the best for this technique. Wax carving tools, which are not too sharp, are ideal for carving cuttlefish. The inside of the bone is the right density for either carving out a pattern, casting a complete sheet of metal, or making an impression of an object. Quite delicate pieces can be produced in this way.

SAND

Casting sand is available from jewelry suppliers. It is a dense, rather oily sand which should be kept in an airtight bag or container to prevent it drying out. Aluminum flasks of different sizes are used for packing the sand, although wooden boxes can be constructed fairly simply if a larger item is required.

Found objects such as wood, stones, shells, beach glass, and plastic or wax models, or anything with an interesting surface, can all be reproduced in this way. It is better to avoid the sand casting method for items with a thickness of less than $^1/_8$ inch/2mm, as the molten metal may not spread to the full extent of the model.

SAFETY

- Secure the two sides of the cuttlefish together with binding wire, to ensure that the model does not have "flashing" at the edges, and that the molten metal does not spill out from the sides.
- Support the cuttlefish between two soldering blocks so that it is stable when molten metal is poured into it.
- Place the cuttlefish or sand container in a tin or soldering table large enough to field any "overspills" of molten metal.
- Wear insulated gloves when undoing containers after pouring in the molten metal.
- Quench the model in water after it has been allowed to cool in the cuttlefish or sand.
- Do not reuse cuttlefish after a casting. Sand which has been burnt around a cast silver piece should be discarded. Clean sand can be reused.

Support the cuttlefish on both sides before casting the molten metal into it.

PREPARING THE METAL

To achieve a good casting, make sure the correct weight of metal is melted. It is difficult to estimate the weight of silver needed to cast, for example, a piece of dry wood. Work on the basis that silver is approximately 11 times the weight of wax to estimate the weight of silver required for casting. If you allow too much metal you will have a very large sprue; if too little, you may only have enough for half your model, which, after pickling, can be melted up again. Whatever weight is estimated, always add a further $^1/_2$ oz/10g to allow for the sprue. This is important as it gives both weight and a reservoir from which the casting can feed. Chop the metal into pieces no larger than $^1/_2$ inch/1cm square and place them in a crucible with a little flux.

CARVED PATTERN CASTING

If the cuttlefish is damp, dry it out slowly before using it for casting.

❶ Use a piercing saw to cut off the top and bottom quarter of the cuttlefish in a straight line. Remove the edge of the hard piece of the bone by cutting down the side of the cuttlefish. Then, as smoothly as possible, cut down through the center so that it is in two halves. Place the two halves together again and strike two locating lines across the top.

Cut down the center of the cuttlefish with the piercing saw.

❷ Start carving approximately 1 inch/2cm down from the top. The carving should flow downward from the top, because it is difficult to get silver to flow backward. Draw some air lines from the carving out toward the edge. From the top, down to the pattern, carve out a V-shaped funnel for the sprue. Cut a similar V-shaped funnel out of the top of the uncarved side of the cuttlefish, to make the sprue entrance as large as possible. The cast silver piece will have a flat back, which takes on the appearance of the cuttlefish.

Pattern and sprue carved out of the cuttlefish, with the sprue cut in the uncarved side of the bone.

❸ Put the two sides back together again and secure with binding wire. Support the cuttlefish between two soldering blocks.

❹ Heat the metal in the crucible until it is molten. Retain it at molten temperature for 20 seconds before holding the crucible over the sprue hole and pouring in the molten metal as quickly and smoothly as possible.

❺ Allow the metal to cool for one minute before opening the cuttlefish. Quench the casting in water. Pickle to remove any oxidization. Pierce through the sprue end to remove it.

Allow the metal to stay in a molten state for 20 seconds before casting into either sand or cuttlefish. It should have a "spinning" appearance. As the crucible is held, agitate it gently forward and backward to ensure the metal runs smoothly.

SAND CASTING

❶ Pack one half of the container with sand and smooth the top. Push the model halfway down into the sand. Brush the top lightly with talcum powder. Place the second half of the container (lining up the location points) on top of the first and pack tightly with sand until it is full.

❷ Use a wooden mallet to compact the sand into the container as tightly as possible. Smooth the top. Separate the two halves. Carefully remove the model from the sand. Make a sprue hole through the top half, directly down onto the model. For larger pieces, two sprue holes may work better. When casting a large piece which is not uniformly round, it is easier to divide the initial sprue in the top container into two as it comes down onto the model.

A piece of flint pressed into the sand to make an impression.

❸ The top opening needs to be large enough to pour in the molten metal and then it should narrow down through the sand so that the point of contact with the back of the model is not too big. Use drill pieces of $^1/_{16}$ to $^1/_8$ inch/2 to 3mm to make sprue lines. Draw air lines in the bottom container, away from the sides of the impression.

❹ Once the sprue holes are clear, the model has been removed, and the air lines have been made, put the two halves back together, lining up the location points.

❺ Cast the molten metal, as in step 4 of Carved Pattern Casting (see previous page)

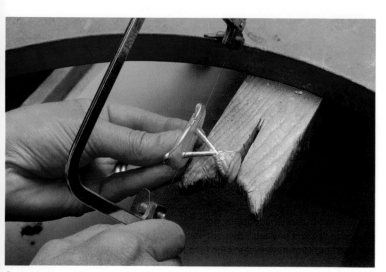

Sprue down to the casting, showing where it was divided in two.

FOUND OBJECT CASTING

A cuttlefish can also be used to cast a three-dimensional object.

❶ After cutting down through the cuttlefish so that it is in two halves, push two small locating pins in one side toward the edges near the top. Push a third pin toward the base. The pins should protrude about $^1/_2$ inch/1cm. Press the second half down onto the locating pins.

❷ Separate the two sides and press the model into one side of the bone about 1 inch/2cm from the top. Press down firmly until half the model has been pushed into the bone. Carve out the sprue V-shape on both sides. Draw air lines out to the edge.

❸ Replace the second half using the location pins as a guide and press the other half of the model in until the two sides fit together again. Open the cuttlefish to remove the model.

❹ Continue from step 3 of Carved Pattern Casting (see previous page).

SAMPLES • Casting

These samples have been cast in either cuttlefish or sand. The main purpose of casting here is both to create a three-dimensional shape, and to create an interesting surface texture on the shape.

HOW THE SAMPLES WERE ACHIEVED

CUTTLEFISH CARVING 1–3

SILVER

❶ Shape carved in the cuttlefish to a depth of ¹/₈ inch/2mm. Lines in the corners carved a deeper ¹/₈ inch/2mm.

❷ Pattern carved to a depth of ¹/₈ inch/2mm. A curved chasing tool used to push out the lines.

❸ Pattern carved to a depth of ¹/₈ inch/2mm, and a small shell pushed several times into the cuttlefish.

SAND CASTING 4–6

SILVER

❹ Pattern first carved in blue wax and then pressed into casting sand.

❺ Pattern carved with engraving tools in green wax—slightly harder than blue—and cast in sand.

❻ Effect created by pushing a brass button into sand. Note the fine detail.

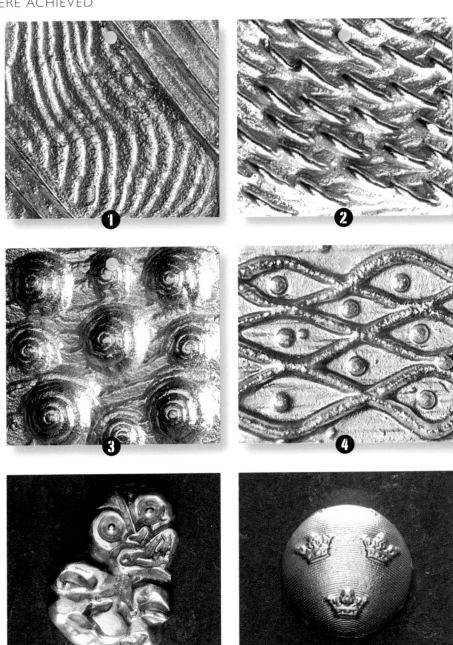

HELPFUL HINTS

- After casting into sand, discard all the burnt sand.
- Don't forget to add at least 10g to the weight of metal you are melting for your casting, to allow for the sprue.
- Store casting sand in an airtight plastic bag. Do not allow it to dry out.
- A mold that makes a clear deep imprint in the sand works better than a very thin one.

- When buying cuttlefish for casting, choose a big fat one and make sure it is dry.
- After use, throw the cuttlefish away. It is not possible to reuse the mold.
- The two halves of the cuttlefish should fit snugly together. If they do not, the cast piece will not be aligned properly.

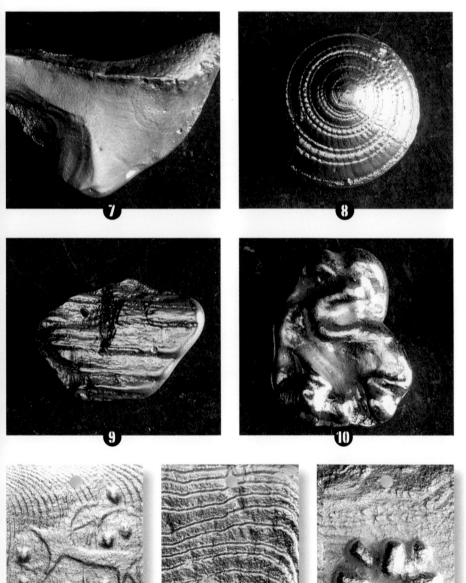

SAND CASTING 7–10
SILVER

❼ Pattern formed when a piece of flint was pressed into sand. As it was a heavy casting, a double sprue was used.

❽ Pattern formed from a sundial shell pushed into sand.

❾ Pattern formed from a piece of broken wood pushed into sand.

❿ Abstract pattern made by holding randomly carved blue wax over a flame to soften the edges, and then pushing it into sand.

CUTTLEFISH CASTING 11–13
SILVER

⓫ Impression made using a bronze button pushed into the cuttlefish.

⓬ Effect created by carving a small square area out of one side of a cuttlefish. This sample shows the really good markings typical of a cuttlefish casting.

⓭ Rosette shape made by pushing a repoussé tool into the cuttlefish.

SHOWCASE • **Casting**

Some of these pieces have been cast using the "lost wax" process which is generally used when casting several identical items. Sand and cuttlefish casting is more suited to one-off pieces or particular parts of a piece. The pieces shown here with sample icons beside them could have been cast in either sand or cuttlefish.

PORTRAIT BROOCH

Margaret Shepherd • Sterling silver and 22-carat gold

The hands and face of this figurative brooch are lost wax cast elements and the main body is repousséd. Etched detail on the skirt, and applied gold decoration contrast with the oxidization to achieve a realistic portrait.

LIGHT IV

Kuo-Jen Chen • 18-carat gold and diamond

Squares have been used as the motif, some set with diamonds, for this delicate pendant, cast in gold using the lost wax process.

POMPOM RINGS

Jo Lavelle • Sterling silver

A multitude of tiny cast elements have been grouped together to form the focal point of these rings, creating a real sense of movement.

CARVED COLLECTION
Mari Thomas • Sterling silver and 18-carat gold
Patination has been used to accentuate the sculptural surfaces on some of the cast pieces within this collection. Variations of form have been used to create a coherent set.

LEAPING SALMON RING
Margaret Shepherd • Sterling silver, 9- and 22-carat gold, and black pearl
This exquisite ring has been modeled in wax, and then cast in silver. Gold has been inlaid and applied to the surface, then the ring has been patinated with a color that complements the pearl.

PEBBLE NECKLACE
Nicola Morris • Sterling silver
The sand cast links of this necklace have been riveted together to form a chain. A satin finish has been applied with fine wire wool, giving each "pebble" a soft, tactile quality.

TWIG PENDANTS
Kyoko Urino • Sterling silver, 18-carat gold, and pearl
Cast twigs have been fabricated into simple triangular forms, one in oxidized silver, the other in burnished gold, and topped with a pearl, to make a pair of beautiful pendants.

TECHNIQUE • **Press forming**

Press forming produces a raised pattern or shape in metal, pushed through from behind. A mold is made, using a "sandwich" of a sheet of metal between two sheets of acrylic, and pressed tightly together in a fly press. The mold can be used many times, making this process both practical and economical.

The press must have two identical steel plates, one for the mold to sit on, and the other to come down with the handle. The acrylic sheet should be at least ¼ inch/4mm thick—any thinner and it may crack under the pressure. Small press-formed pieces can be made using a large vise as a press. Steel plates are necessary for holding the mold and to distribute the pressure, while the vise jaws need rubber or wooden covers to protect the steel plates.

Copper, brass, gilding metal, silver, and gold are suitable metals. Texturing can be done before pressing, but there is likely to be a small amount of distortion due to the pressure during the forming.

PRESS FORMING EQUIPMENT
① *Tracing paper*
② *Sheet of acrylic*
③ *Steel sheet*
④ *Rubber sheet*

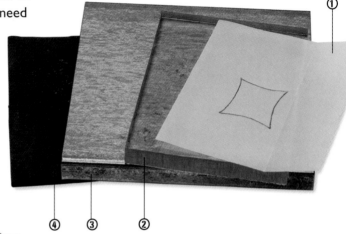

MAKING THE MOLD

This example makes a simple cushion shape, to show how easily other shapes can be made.

❶ For a metal cushion measuring 1 x ⅞ inches/2.5 x 2.2cm, a sheet of acrylic of 2 x 2 inches/5 x 5cm is required.

❷ Mark the center point. Scribe a horizontal and a vertical line through the acrylic sheet. Use the center point of the sheet as the center of the cushion. Scribe the shape.

❸ Drill a hole, no larger than ¹/₁₆ inch/1mm diameter, anywhere on the scribed line of the cushion shape.

❹ Thread a piercing saw through the hole and cut out the shape around the line.

❺ Shape the two pieces of acrylic sheet as "male" (the cushion piece) and "female" (the piece the cushion was cut from). The "male" will have a scribed line forming a cross on the top surface. File the "male" cushion to shape from the underneath surface. Start with a fairly coarse file and clean up with a finer file and wet-and-dry papers until a smooth shape is achieved.

❻ Now file the "female." With a pair of dividers set at ¹/₈ or ³/₁₆ inch/3 or 4mm, use the edge of the cut-out area as the guide, and scribe a line round the outside edge. Take an oval file and file a slant up to the scribed line and down to the back. The curve of the "female" should correspond with that of the "male." The mold is now ready for use.

File and smooth the "male" pattern so that the metal being formed is pushed evenly into place. Clean the "female" piece in the same way.

PRESSING

1 Take a piece of metal $1^5/_8$ x $1^1/_4$ inch x 0.6mm/4 x 3cm x 0.6mm. Carry out any texturing work necessary before the pressing. Anneal the piece.

2 Mark the center point and lightly scribe the horizontal and vertical lines through the center point.

3 Place the metal on top of the "female" and line up horizontal and vertical lines. Tape down the corners of the metal to the acrylic sheet. Line up the "male" on top of the metal and tape down.

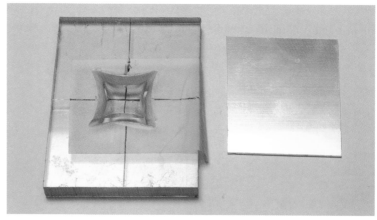

Fit the "male" and "female" together and draw horizontal and vertical lines across both before adding the metal.

4 Check everything is aligned and tape the whole thing to the steel base plate.

5 Bring the top plate down to press onto the bottom, by swinging the handle down and around. If the pressing is being done in a vise, close the vise carefully until "male" and "female" converge. This means that the metal has been squeezed down into the space made between them. Undo the vise and remove the piece.

6 Pierce away any extra metal around the edge of the shape.

The silver is held in place across the "female" piece and the "male" piece is lined up and held in place with masking tape.

A small hydraulic press which is levered upward. Pressure is put on the two stainless-steel plates so that the "male" piece is pressed into the "female" piece. The metal being held between the two is pushed down.

SAFETY

- Care must be taken that there is nothing in the way as the handle of the press turns. Some presses have large, heavy handles which swing down when pressure is applied.
- When a press is not in use, remove the handle and store it elsewhere.

SAMPLES • **Press forming**

Press forming is an excellent technique for repeating a three-dimensional shape. It is usually done with either an old-fashioned "fly press" or a smaller hydraulic press but it is also possible to press form simply by squeezing the work tightly in a large vise.

HOW THE SAMPLES WERE ACHIEVED

SUBSTRATE 1-4

GILDING METAL

❶ Effect of a triangle within a circle achieved by pressing a circle made from acrylic sheet, and then placing a ³/₈ inch/4mm rubber sheet behind the circle and pressing a triangle, also made from acrylic sheet, through it.

❷ Effect achieved by pressing a circle made from acrylic sheet, placing a ³/₈ inch/4mm rubber sheet behind the circular pressing, and then pressing an inner circle through from the top with another acrylic former.

❸ Simple shape formed using an acrylic sheeting male/female pressing.

❹ Effect achieved by first using a male/female acrylic sheet former and the framework around it, then cutting out the reverse in stainless steel and pressing it again.

❺ More complicated shapes such as this starfish can also be achieved with acrylic sheet formers. Note the creasing at the edges created by the pressing, which adds to the interest.

SUBSTRATE 5-6

COPPER

❻ Annealed metal passed through a rolling mill (see page 20) to imprint "tadpole" shapes cut from stainless steel. The metal was annealed and press formed in a male/female mold.

❼ Annealed metal passed through a rolling mill along with some lace fabric, and then heated to 1,652°F/900°C to achieve color. A round mold with an oval center was used to press the shape.

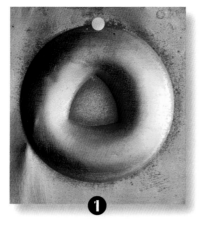

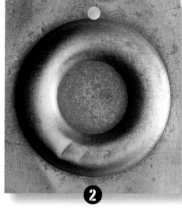

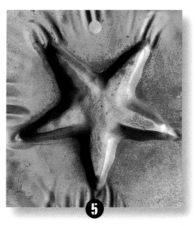

HELPFUL HINTS

- To prevent any cracking when under pressure in the press, make sure that the acrylic sheet, from which the male and female molds are made, has an area away from the pattern edge of at least 1³/₁₆ inch/3cm.
- Anneal any metal to be press formed.

- Try to use sheet metal of 0.5mm or less in thickness. Thicker metal will be more difficult to shape without creasing.
- For a smooth result, file the sides of the acrylic sheet male and female molds. Finish with wet-and-dry papers.

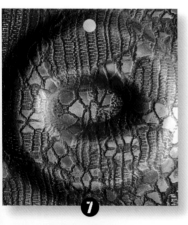

SUBSTRATE 7–11

SILVER

8 Flower pattern cut from stainless steel and passed through a rolling mill on the silver, three times, to make the impression. The imprint was then pressed through an oval former.

9 The central cross was rolled into the metal before a double pressing. First, an outer circle of solid acrylic sheet was used. Next, another outer circle was used, but this time with a hollow center into which was fitted an inner circle twice the depth of the outer. The central cross was then decorated with fused gold leaf.

10 Cushion-shape made by male/female acrylic sheet formers.

11 Silver passed through a rolling mill with open-weave fabric, annealed and pressed into a oval dome using a male/female acrylic sheet former.

SUBSTRATE 12

BRASS

12 Main circle pressed with a male/female acrylic sheet former. A triangular center was used for the second pressing and the outer circle was kept in shape by placing a wire ring into it as the triangle was pressed through.

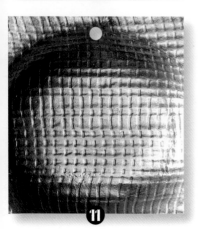

It's difficult to believe that all these designs were created using the same technique. For some pieces, such as the feather pod necklace, *Daybreak I*, *Stars II*, and the multi necklace, further decoration was added either before or after the basic shape was formed. For the *Leaf* collection, however, the surface decoration was applied as part of the press forming process.

LONG FEATHER POD NECKPIECE

Shimara Carlow • Sterling silver

Many units have been assembled to make this stunning neckpiece. Feathers have been roller-printed onto sheet silver which has then been press formed, giving a delicate texture to each unit.

REVOLUTION II

Kuo-Jen Chen • 18-carat gold and lacquer
Press forms are the basis for this neckpiece of repeated forms, which have been skillfully linked together with large gold wire circles.

LEAF BANGLES

Naomi James • Sterling silver
A rusty hammer has provided texture on the body of these bangles, that have been embossed with a steel template in the fly-press.

DAYBREAK I

Kuo-Jen Chen • Sterling silver,
lacquer, and 18-carat gold
*The volume of this circular
pendant has been optimized
by the striking effect of lacquer
on the surface and the
polished silver inner ring.*

STARS II

Kuo-Jen Chen • Sterling
silver and lacquer
*Press forms have been
linked together to form a
bold neckpiece composed
of squares.*

MULTI NECKLACE

Jinks McGrath • Sterling silver
and 22-carat gold
*This effective necklace is
composed of graduated
press formed units, containing
gold discs, enameled discs,
and tourmalines. The silver has
been given a textured matt
finish for more interest.*

LEAF COLLECTION

Naomi James • Sterling silver,
18-carat gold, and garnet
*The raised leaf patterns have
been embossed using a steel
template, and the beads have
been press formed to create
volume. Gold details add interest
to this collection.*

TECHNIQUE • **Reticulation**

The decorative effect of reticulation can be confused with that of fusing (see page 28) as the surface movement in both techniques looks similar. However, there are distinct differences that affect how the finished piece appears and is used.

Unlike fused metal, where the surface has a slightly heavier and more porous appearance and the movement occurs on the surface, the surface of reticulated metal does not appear porous. Despite undulations, the surface remains intact and all movement occurs under the surface, presenting a raised and wavy appearance.

Shape reticulated metal carefully as thickness variations may occur. It is sometimes better to shape the metal first and then reticulate it. As the variation in the thickness is unpredictable, there may also be breakthrough in the surface. This, however, can be put to good use by inserting a stone or decoration.

Standard silver and some gold can be reticulated, although an alloy of 82 per cent silver and 18 per cent copper produces the best results. As this is below sterling quality, it must be used as an insert and not soldered to anything of sterling quality.

RETICULATION EQUIPMENT
① *Flat soldering block to keep the silver flat during the process*
② *Charcoal soldering block (good heat reflection properties)*

PREPARING THE SURFACE
Use metal with a minimum thickness of $^1/_{16}$ inch/1mm.

❶ Begin with a sheet of standard silver measuring 3 x 2$^1/_2$ x $^1/_{16}$ inches/ 8 x 6cm x 1.2mm. Place the metal on a flat soldering block. Use the block throughout to ensure that the hot metal does not droop or melt when in an unsupported position.

❷ Heat the metal to annealing temperature, which is visible when the metal glows dull red. Use a soft oxidizing flame and play it over the surface for about 15 seconds at this temperature (no hotter) before quenching and pickling. Do not remove the piece from the pickle until the surface looks "white."

Anneal the silver at least seven times. The more it is annealed, the less oxidization will appear. After three or four annealings, the silver should remain white during subsequent heating.

SAFETY

- Use either a soldering block or charcoal block, placed on a soldering table, when annealing and reticulating.
- Some parts of the reticulated sheet may be thin and therefore sharp. Take care when piercing out any shapes from the finished sheet.

❸ Repeat the process seven times. As each annealing takes place it becomes more difficult to see the color that was so obvious at the first heating. Look at the edges to see them become red at the same time as seeing a dull red appearing under the "white" of the surface. If the heat is too strong, dark areas of oxidization will break through this surface, and the sequence must be begun again.

❹ During repeated pickling, the surface is stripped of its copper content, leaving a thin outer layer of "white" pure silver. As the layer builds up, the alloy containing the copper is "pushed" down into the center of the piece.

❺ After the piece has been annealed for a seventh time, it is ready to be reticulated.

After several annealings, it becomes more difficult to know when the required heat has been reached. Look carefully to see the faint pink color that appears under the white surface and on the edges of the metal. This indicates that the annealing temperature has been reached.

At the final heating, a second flame is introduced. The first flame keeps the whole piece at a constant temperature, while the second plays up and down the piece to form the pattern.

RETICULATING SILVER

❶ Heat the silver as before, but to a slightly higher temperature. While one torch holds it at the temperature, introduce another torch with a harder, more directional flame.

❷ Move the flame back and forward over the metal until the surface has a "sea"-like appearance. The surface should start to move with an increase in heat. If it breaks through, pull the flame away until the shininess disappears and then gradually apply it again.

The pattern has started to appear. The second flame keeps working around the silver to form the pattern.

Once the silver has been pickled, clean it with a brass brush and liquid soap.

❸ Once the piece is reticulated, allow it to cool for 30 seconds before quenching and giving it a good pickle. Clean it with a pumice powder paste or a brass brush with liquid soap. It is quite usual for some areas to look better than others. Cut out the preferred area and use it as the base for the piece.

SAMPLES • **Reticulation**

These samples demonstrate the recognizable effects of reticulation. However, it is practically impossible to recreate any of the samples exactly—a different pattern appears every time a piece is reticulated. The more thorough the annealing and pickling process is, the better the result.

HOW THE SAMPLES WERE ACHIEVED

SUBSTRATE 1-5

SILVER

❶ Markings typical of reticulation were achieved when silver was annealed and pickled seven times.

❷ Silver was subjected to three annealings and picklings. As the fourth annealing began, this reticulation began to appear.

❸ A sheet of silver was first textured with fabric through a rolling mill, and then annealed and pickled four times. Reticulation began on the fifth heating.

❹ Reticulation was achieved as in sample 1 above and beautiful undulations resulted. 24-carat gold was fused after reticulation.

❺ Classic reticulation markings were achieved as in sample 1 above and the piece was oxidized afterward to give the blue/pink effect. The relief areas were polished with a buffing cloth.

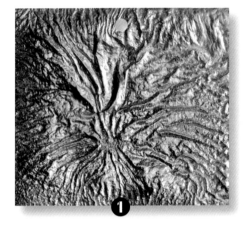

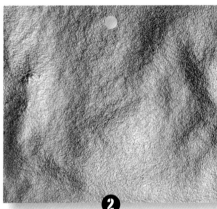

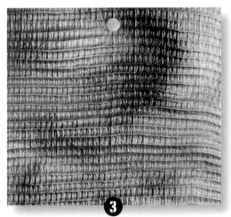

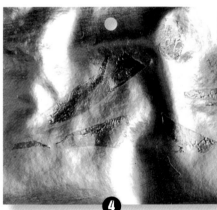

HELPFUL HINTS

- Reticulation works better on smaller pieces, ideally no bigger than 3⅜ inches/8cm².
- Reticulation results are unpredictable; it is best to design your piece around a finished piece of reticulated metal rather than attempting to reticulate a design later.
- Note that the thickness of the finished reticulated sheet will vary, depending on how the heat has affected it.

- If you want to solder a collet for a stone onto the sheet, you may find it easier to cut out the shape of the collet in the sheet before soldering it in.
- Clean a reticulated sheet by scrubbing vigorously with a brass brush and liquid soap.
- When heating the metal for reticulation, lay it flat on a soldering block. If any part of the metal is unsupported, it will slump during the process.

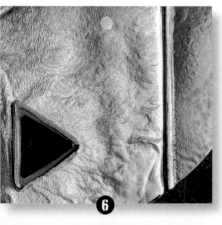

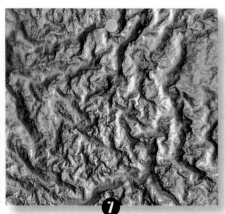

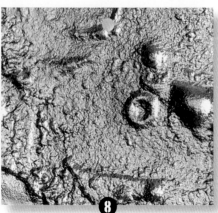

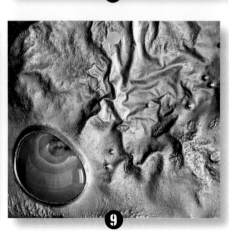

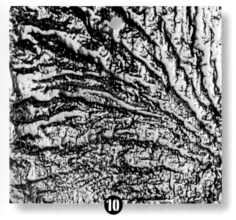

SUBSTRATE 6-9

SILVER

6 After reticulation, as in sample 1, the right-hand section was taken from a different area, shaped to fit and soldered to the main piece with a delineating piece of gold. The gold setting was prepared for a faceted stone.

7 An alloy of 82 per cent silver and 18 per cent copper has produced excellent reticulation, using the same method as in sample 1.

8 As this piece was being reticulated, small pieces were added until they fused with the metal.

9 The stone was set by cutting the shape out of the reticulated sheet, to allow the setting to slip in and then be soldered in position.

SUBSTRATE 10

GOLD

10 A sheet of 9-carat gold shows classic reticulation markings. Results with 9-carat gold can be unpredictable, and sometimes may not "take" at all.

SHOWCASE • **Reticulation**

The effect of reticulation is as though someone has picked up a piece of metal, screwed it into a ball like a piece of paper, and then straightened it out. Unfortunately it's not as easy as that and reticulating a large piece of silver successfully takes some practice! These pieces are all good examples; the way light plays around them is particularly effective.

CRACKED DOME NECKLACE

Anne Morgan • Sterling silver
Press forming and soldering have been combined with reticulation to create this intriguing cracked silver sphere.

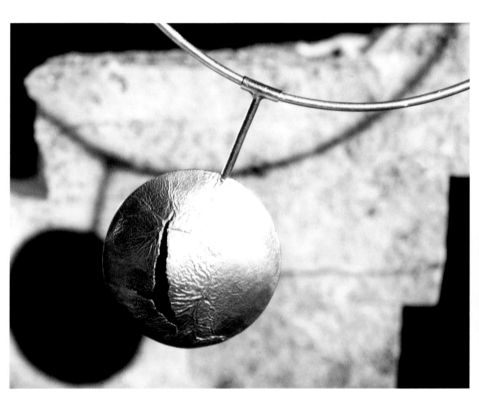

LARGE DAISY NECKPIECE

Shimara Carlow • Sterling silver
Reticulation has been used on domed silver discs to recreate the delicate texture of petals, giving this neckpiece an organic quality.

STRUCTURED RINGS

Anne Morgan • Sterling silver and 18-carat gold
*The designer has reticulated the silver bands of these
rings and contrasted this with differing structural gold
wire to make a stylish collection.*

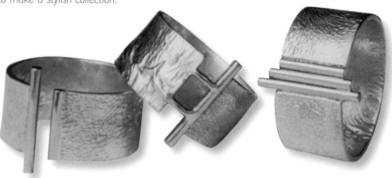

CURVED BANGLE

Jean Scott-Moncrieff • Sterling silver and 18-carat gold
*The abstract pattern on this bangle has been made with
applied gold spirals on a reticulated ground to give detail to
a bold form.*

TECHNIQUE • **Gold and silver foil**

Applying very delicate pieces of gold and silver to a contrasting metal is known as "keum-boo." The process originates from Korea where 24-carat gold foil was used to decorate brass and silver vessels. 23.5-carat gold and fine silver foil can be bought in "leaves" from bullion suppliers, in differing millimeter thicknesses. Other gold foils, called "leaf", are more often used for gilding wooden frames and are not suitable for keum-boo as they are too thin and tend to disappear into the parent metal, leaving a green trace. It is possible to use 24-carat gold that is slightly thicker, to give a more definite look, and it pays to experiment with different thickness to find what is most suitable.

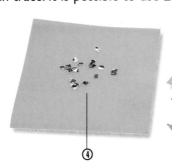

FOIL EQUIPMENT
① *Gold foil on tracing paper*
② *Small soft brush*
③ *Scalpel*
④ *Gold foil cut into small squares with a craft knife*

METAL PREPARATION

Access to a rolling mill is required to make foil from sheet. 24-carat gold sheet and fine silver are both suitable to roll down. If they start to harden during the process, they can be annealed, pickled, and rinsed in the usual way. When the sheet has been rolled down to 0.1mm, it may be necessary to place it between sheets of tracing paper and roll it down further to get to a finished thickness of 0.01 or 0.02mm.

The parent metal should be free of any oxidization. If attaching gold foil to silver sheet, the silver should be annealed and pickled a minimum of three or four times in order to build up a thin coat of fine white silver. This can then be cleaned gently with a brush and soapy water and dried.

Gold foil can be applied when the metal is in sheet form, or on a finished article. Soldering the sheet with the fused foil too many times during subsequent fabrication can cause the gold to fade. However, the gold will not deteriorate if it is applied to a finished item and then re-soldered.

APPLYING GOLD FOIL

❶ Place one piece of gold foil between two sheets of tracing paper and draw the required shape onto the paper. Place the "sandwich" onto a rubber cutting board and cut round the tracing with a craft knife. Do not try to place too large a piece of gold foil on at any one time.

❷ Apply a little saliva onto the parent surface where the foil is to be placed. Lift the cut-out pattern of gold from the paper with a small, damp paintbrush. Avoid touching the foil by hand during the process. Gently lay the foil down and brush over the top of the surface with the paintbrush, to remove any air bubbles that may be trapped underneath it.

SAFETY

● Use a sharp craft knife to cut the foil through the tracing paper.
● Always follow the cutting line away from you and make sure that the knife cannot suddenly slip into a supporting finger.

Pick up the tiny pieces of gold with the end of a damp paintbrush and place them onto the silver. The paintbrush is also used to push the gold pieces gently down into place.

❸ Have a small stainless-steel burnisher at hand. Bring the heat onto the piece slowly, taking care to keep the flame away from the foil as much as possible. The flame should be aimed at the metal and brought to annealing temperature (a soft pink color will show around the edges and through the white of the silver). Maintain the heat of the flame with one hand, while using the burnisher in the other hand to very gently touch the center of the foil. If the foil stays attached to the metal, continue with the burnisher, gently pressing the foil down to cover the designated area. If the foil starts to lift off apply a little more heat, before trying the burnisher again.

❹ Once the foil is in place, quench and pickle the piece. If any more foil needs to be added, repeat the process as desired.

❺ Gently brush the piece with a glass brush or fine steel wool and soap. The gold foil can be highlighted with a burnisher, as can the background metal if desired. It is preferable not to finish with a mop on the polishing machine as the gold will disappear if any pressure is applied. Rolled-down, 0.1mm thick gold can be polished gently on the polishing machine.

As the silver reaches annealing temperature, introduce a burnisher to carefully rub the gold foil down onto it.

For a frosted finish to the gold foil, put the piece, with the gold fused into position, through the rolling mill with some wet-and-dry paper.

DEWDROPS BY NIGHT FRUIT TRAY
Kuo-Jen Chen
Gold foil has been applied over a dark red lacquer to enhance the organic appearance of this unique fruit tray.

SAMPLES • **Gold and silver foil**

Adding gold or silver foil to a piece can totally transform it. Use foil to enhance raised areas or delineate embossed lines. Wrap it around wire, tuck it down into etched areas, or burnish it into the detail of a reticulated piece. Using foil on a piece of metal before oxidizing produces a fantastic effect as the foil itself does not oxidize, offering a strong contrast.

HOW THE SAMPLES WERE ACHIEVED

SUBSTRATE 1-5

SILVER

❶ Silver was reticulated and cleaned thoroughly with fine steel wool and liquid soap. Gold foil was placed onto the silver with saliva and heated to annealing temperature. A burnisher was used to gently rub the gold down onto the silver background.

❷ Silver was enameled with transparent purple and fired when cool. Silver foil was brushed onto the surface. The piece was refired in same conditions as for the enamel and a burnisher was used to rub it gently as it was removed from the kiln.

❸ Silver was textured through a rolling mill with fabric. Small gold foil squares were paintbrushed onto the surface and then heated to annealing temperature before being burnished on.

❹ Silver was textured through a rolling mill with fabric and then gently reticulated. The gold foil diamond shape was paintbrushed onto the surface with saliva and heated again to annealing temperature. The gold was burnished onto the silver at this heat.

❺ The cast was achieved by cuttlefish carving. Gold foil was placed in the grooves and the piece was heated from behind until the foil could be burnished onto the silver.

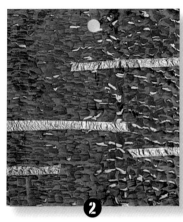

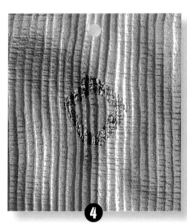

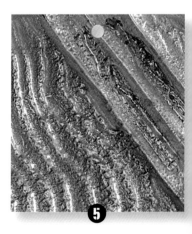

HELPFUL HINTS

- When cutting shapes out of foil, place the foil between two sheets of tracing paper, and cut out the shape with a sharp craft knife.
- Use a fine paintbrush and saliva to lift foil—try not to handle it with your fingers.
- Only use "foil." Silver and gold "leaf" is different and too fine to heat onto a metal surface.

- For pieces of foil larger than $3/8$ inch/1cm^2, use the end of a fine pin to prick some tiny holes in the foil. This will help it stay flat while being heated.
- Avoid allowing the flame to touch the foil directly until you are sure it has adhered to the surface of the metal. The flame will make the foil curl up making it impossible to burnish flat.

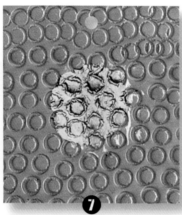

SUBSTRATE 6-7

SILVER

❻ A cast piece was decorated with gold foil round the base of the top area. After fusing, a glass brush was used over the whole piece to remove some gold foil, to give the effect of gold "painted" onto the surface.

❼ The pattern was achieved using a round stamping tool. Gold foil was placed in the center and fused on at annealing temperature. The foil follows the contours of the pattern.

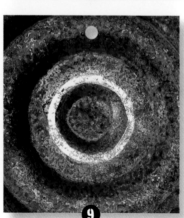

SUBSTRATE 8-10

COPPER

❽ A diamond impression was made in annealed copper. Another diamond shape was cut out of gold foil and inserted in the indentation. The piece was heated to annealing temperature and the gold rubbed with a burnisher to fix it in place.

❾ Borax was painted over the surface to keep the copper coloring, except where silver foil was placed. It was heated from behind and, when hot enough, the silver foil was rubbed down with a burnisher.

❿ Silver and gold foil were paintbrushed with saliva onto etched copper. The piece was heated and, when hot enough, the gold and silver foil were rubbed down with a burnisher. The three colors, plus the variety of color produced by the etching and heating, create a "geographic" effect.

SHOWCASE • **Gold and silver foil**

The pieces in this showcase would look completely different without the gold and silver decoration. Tiny pieces of gold or silver foil, placed in the perfect position, can transform a piece of jewelry into something really special. This can be central to the design, as seen in the sundrops necklace, or used to delicately illuminate as in the twig bangle.

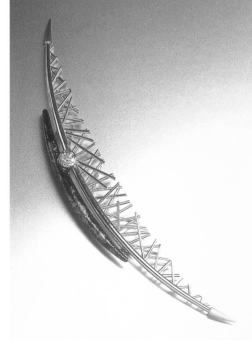

GOLD PATTERNED BROOCHES
Chris Carpenter • Sterling silver, 22-carat gold, and gilding metal
Gold foil has been used to emphasize and pick out areas of the roller-printed patterns, and add diversity to this collection of brooches that explores the effect of color and pattern on form.

MOONLIGHT BROOCH
Kuo-Jen Chen • 18-carat gold and metal foil, diamond, and lacquer
Yellow gold foil has been applied to emphasize an area of this radiant white-gold brooch.

4 **7**

SUNDROPS NECKLACE
Emma Gale • Mother-of-pearl, gold foil, and nylon
Gold foil has been applied to mother-of-pearl discs in this delicate multi-stranded necklace.

10

SQUARE SILVER BROOCH
EM Jewellery • Sterling silver and precious metal foil
Precious metal foil has been fused onto one half of this brooch, giving a colorful contrast to the brushed silver surface.

9

TWIG BANGLE
Kyoko Urino • Copper and gold foil
The designer has used delicate application of gold foil to highlight areas of the electroformed twigs, which have also been patinated.

TECHNIQUE • **Granulation**

Granulation was used by the Etruscans and the ancient Greeks to decorate pieces of pure gold, for *objets d'art* and jewelry. It is a surface decoration made by applying tiny balls, usually of 22- or 24-carat gold, onto a background. It is most often seen today in jewelry from the Indian sub-continent, which is highly prized for its extravagant use of gold.

True granulation (the organic glue methods described here) uses a fusion-welding action to attach the balls to the background metal. A medium of organic glue and copper is placed between the base of the gold ball and the gold background. It is then heated with an oxidizing flame to a temperature at which the glue carbonizes and lowers the melting temperature of the copper, to combine with both gold surfaces to fuse them together.

Use high-carat gold or fine silver granules when working with the organic glue methods. Standard silver may be used when working with the filed solder method.

GRANULATION EQUIPMENT
① Silver wire
② Charcoal powder
③ Auflux
④ Borax cone
⑤ Lengths of solder
⑥ Flat file

MAKING THE BALLS

❶ Decide what size and roughly how many balls the pattern will require. To make the balls of equal size, take some 0.5mm silver wire and cut pieces of equal length, for example, ¹/₈ inch/4mm each. You may want to mix silver with gold and vary the sizes. To make larger balls, cut longer lengths of wire. To make smaller balls, ¹/₁₆ inch/2mm x 0.5mm round wire would be appropriate.

❷ Place each length of wire into holes made in a charcoal soldering block. Heat each piece of wire until it melts and forms into a ball. Allow it to spin for a few seconds before moving onto the next piece.

❸ Clean the balls by placing them in a small container filled with pickle and then put the container into the warm pickle.

❹ To make several balls simultaneously, place loose powdered charcoal in the bottom of a container suitable for use in a hot kiln. Place equal-sized pieces of silver or gold wire on top of the charcoal, equally spaced. Sprinkle another layer of charcoal on top (deep enough to prevent metal pieces falling through) and then place more pieces of metal on the charcoal, and so on, for four layers. Finish with a final layer of charcoal.

❺ Heat a kiln to 1,652°F/900°C for silver and 2,012°F/1,100°C for gold, and place the container in the kiln for 15 to 30 minutes, depending on the size of the container. Remove from the kiln and allow to cool.

Make small holes in a charcoal block using a drill and place pieces of gold wire into them.

SAFETY

• Work in a well-ventilated area when using chemicals. Use rubber gloves if possible and wash your hands after use.

ATTACHING THE BALLS

There are two methods of attaching decorative balls to the base: a) using filed solder, where the solder reaches around the base of the ball to give a much wider joining area, rather than it appearing as if the balls are balancing; or b) using organic glue.

Use fine stainless steel tweezers to pick up the tiny gold balls.

Use a coarse file to make tiny pieces of hard, medium, or easy solder.

USING FILED SOLDER:

❶ Take a 2 inch/5cm length of hard solder and a coarse, flat file, and file some of the solder onto some white paper.

❷ Roll a length of hard solder until it is about half its original thickness. With a pair of snips, cut five or six lengths to within ¹/₄ inch/5mm of the top. Use some top cutters to cut tiny lines across the solder to make very small paillons.

❸ Draw out the pattern on the sheet to which the balls are to be attached. It helps to make a slight depression, with the tip of a drill bit or a graver, for the ball to balance in.

❹ Mix borax with a drop of liquid soap to make a sticky flux. Put a tiny bit of flux where each ball is to be positioned. Pick up the balls with tweezers and place them in position. If there are lots of balls very close together it is easier to use the "filed" solder, which is picked up between the thumb and index finger and scattered over the whole area. If just a few balls are used, place a little solder against each ball so that it touches the ball and the base.

❺ Introduce a very soft flame to allow the flux to dry and all the balls to settle in place before increasing the heat to soldering temperature.

❻ Quench and pickle the piece. Pick up any balls that may have come off. Pickle them in a container and repeat the process until they are all safely soldered on.

USING ORGANIC GLUE:

❶ Mix together a liquid solution of two drops of a high-temperature liquid flux, such as "Auflux", two drops of organic glue (such as gum arabic or gum tragacanth), and 10 drops of water.

❷ Coat 22-carat gold or fine silver balls with a layer of "copper" by placing them in warm pickle along with some iron binding wire and copper until they are copper-plated. Remove the balls from the pickle, rinse very well, and dry.

❸ Pick up the balls with a fine brush using the organic glue solution and place them into position on the surface of the parent 22-carat gold or fine silver. Leave to dry thoroughly (under a lamp to speed the process).

❹ Deploy a gentle (reducing) flame around the whole piece, bringing the heat up beyond annealing temperature. Watch carefully at this stage to see the organic glue blacken and burn away. Continue heating past soldering temperature to fusion temperature (that is, a sudden flash as the surface of the metal starts to melt) and remove the flame quickly. Do not quench. Pickle in the usual way. Use a plastic strainer to catch any granules that have not fused as they fall off in the pickle, and replace them in their correct positions, then repeat the whole procedure.

AN ALTERNATIVE ORGANIC GLUE METHOD:

Instead of placing the balls in pickle with binding wire (to coat them with a layer of copper), they can be dipped in a copper sulfate paste. Thoroughly mix together equal parts of powdered organic glue (mixed with a little water until it forms a creamy consistency), borax powder, and copper sulfate granules.

Dip each ball into the paste and place on the base sheet. Heat until the granulation flash occurs.

Balls placed using the organic glue method will appear as though they are lightly balancing on the base.

SAMPLES • **Granulation**

These granulation samples use either solder or true granulation. Although it may be difficult to see the difference here, a ball that is granulated with solder has a broader attachment area than a ball placed with true granulation. However, either method will produce some lovely surface decoration.

HOW THE SAMPLES WERE ACHIEVED

SUBSTRATE 1-2

COPPER

❶ Silver balls were placed into a diamond-shaped indentation lined with previously run hard solder. The balls were dipped in borax and the piece heated until the solder ran again, fixing the balls in place.

❷ A wire-patterned indentation was made in the metal. Graded silver balls were dipped in a gum arabic-copper sulfate-borax solution and placed into the indentation. The piece was heated until the granulation "flash" occurred.

SUBSTRATE 3-4

STANDARD SILVER

❸ Different size silver balls were placed in tiny indents made in silver with a round-headed punch. Each ball was soldered using a tiny piece of solder.

❹ This was made as a casting model. Each ball was soldered in place.

SUBSTRATE 5-6

FINE SILVER

❺ A scribe was used to outline the star pattern and small balls were dipped in a gum arabic-copper sulfate-borax solution and placed on the scribed line. Larger balls were also dipped in solution and placed on the tips of each point. The piece was heated until the granulation "flash" occurred.

❻ An impression of the shape was made using a template run through a rolling mill. The balls were dipped in a gum arabic-copper sulfate-borax solution and placed into the imprint. The piece was heated until the granulation "flash" occurred.

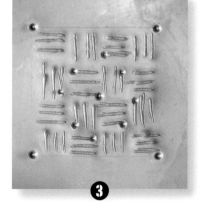
❶

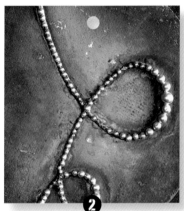
❷

❹

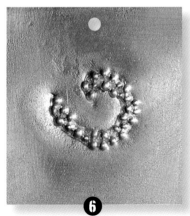
❸

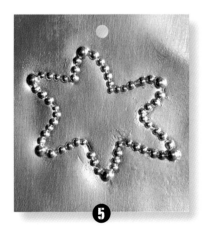
❺

❻

HELPFUL HINTS

- It is a good idea to make lots of balls at one time. Sort them into different sizes if necessary and keep them in separate plastic bags.
- If fusing with filed solder, rather than painting flux on the piece and then sprinkling the filings on, mix powdered flux with the filings and sprinkle on together for a more consistent mix.
- Work on a surface with a raised edge, such as a soldering table, so that any balls which roll off the piece do not disappear onto the floor.
- Make gold and silver balls separately to prevent any mixing of metals at the melting stage.

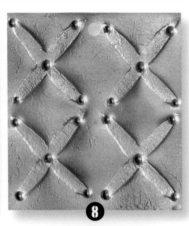

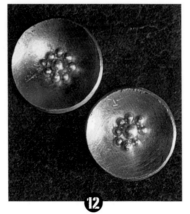

SUBSTRATE 7-11

FINE SILVER

7 Effect achieved following the method used in samples 5 and 6. After the granulation "flash," the piece was quenched and pickled and gold foil applied using a paintbrush and saliva. It was heated to annealing temperature until the gold foil burnished in place.

8 The criss-cross effect was achieved using a rolling mill with a template of the cross pattern. The balls were dipped in a gum-copper sulfate-borax solution, placed in position, and then heated until the granulation "flash" occurred.

9 Graded balls were dipped in a gum-copper sulfate-borax solution and placed in a circle. The granulation "flash" attached the balls to the background and can be seen between each ball.

10 Balls of different sizes were dipped in a gum-copper sulfate-borax solution and placed on a background in a diamond pattern. The piece was heated until the granulation "flash" occurred. Compare the effect of soldering in sample 1, and the effect of true granulation in this sample.

11 A triangular shape was engraved in silver into which fit 18-carat gold balls. Hard solder was run into the triangle first, and then each ball was dipped in borax. The whole piece was heated from underneath to make the solder run.

SUBSTRATE 12

GOLD

12 Domed circles of 22-carat gold were dipped in a gum arabic-copper sulfate-borax solution. The piece was heated until the granulation "flash" occurred.

SHOWCASE • **Granulation**

In essence, granulation decorates a surface with little round balls. But how beautiful and varied these little balls can be! Used to completely cover a surface, placed to perfectly accent a design, or arranged with military precision, the effects can be stunning.

HEAVENLY BODIES II
Kuo-Jen Chen • Sterling silver and lacquer
Fine granulation has been used to embellish the delicate surface of this beautiful pendant.

GRANULATED RINGS
Linda Lewin • 22-carat gold and Britannia silver
Fine granules completely cover these rings.

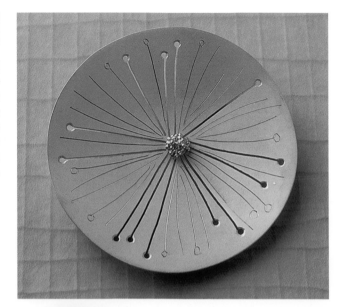

POLLEN BROOCH

Emma Gale • Sterling silver
and 18-carat gold
*The granulated central piece
forms a focal point in this
circular brooch. Decoration has
been made using saw piercing,
drilled holes, and scribed lines.*

OPAL RINGS

Linda Lewin • 22- and
18-carat gold, and opals
*Granulation has been used
as a feature to frame the
settings for these two
luscious opals that adorn
the gold rings.*

MIST BY NIGHT I

Kuo-Jen Chen • Sterling
silver and lacquer
*Granules have been used
to represent stars within
a landscape in this
striking brooch.*

SHIELD BROOCHES

Linda Lewin • Sterling silver, Britannia silver,
18-carat gold, tourmaline, garnet, and amethyst
*The granulated pattern on these three brooches
has been delicately applied in Britannia silver,
giving an effective raised texture that
borders the cabochon gems.*

STEMS BROOCH

Emma Gale • Sterling silver and 18-carat gold
*The designer has used gold balls to add dimension
and color contrast to this brooch. The gold has
been riveted onto sheet metal and each ball has
been supported by an elegantly scribed stem.*

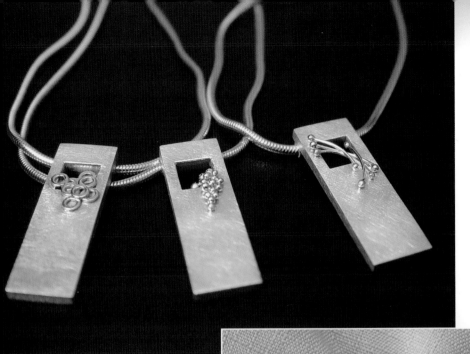

RECTANGLE PENDANTS

EM Jewellery • Sterling silver and 18-carat yellow gold
These pendants demonstrate how granulation can be achieved effectively with small shapes applied to a base. The matt finish of the rectangles gives contrast to the shininess of the granulated areas.

AQUAMARINE BROOCH

Harriet St Leger • 18-carat gold and aquamarine
Graduated gold granules have been soldered onto a gold base to radiate out from a large central stone at the focal point of this distinctive brooch.

CLUSTER I, II & III

Kuo-Jen Chen • Sterling silver and lacquer
The way the rings are displayed makes the tiny granules in the lacquered domes appear to be subject to gravity.

TECHNIQUE • Enameling

Of all the decorative techniques, enameling offers the widest choice in terms of color. It is a truly wonderful medium for expressing ideas and design, and creates endless opportunities for creating patterns in both color and cloisonné wirework.

Enamels give a vibrant finish to work, or are used with great effect in a very subtle way to give just a hint of color. They can be used to create a "stained glass window" effect or to look like a painted picture. The brightness of the metal behind the enamel is used with transparent enamels to give a feeling of depth and quality to the color. Opaque enamels are used to give a richness of color on metal that cannot be achieved in any other way.

Enameling is time-consuming, so a decision to enamel needs to be taken carefully, with as much information available as possible. As this is a book about decorative techniques and not specifically about enameling, please refer to the list of further reading (see page 128) for a fuller picture of the different enameling techniques.

High-carat golds, copper, and silver are suitable media for enameling. Gilding metal can also be enameled provided the percentage of zinc is low enough (under 10 per cent). Steel is also suitable for large decorative purposes, such as panels. Steel is usually purchased with a pre-fired base coat of enamel. Enamels on copper can be fired very successfully with a torch, but generally enamel on silver or gold is best fired in a kiln. The different enameling techniques are described right.

ENAMELING EQUIPMENT
① *Goose quill*
② *Palette with dry ground enamels*
③ *Pestle and mortar*
④ *Paintbrushes*
⑤ *Lumps of transparent enamels*

SAFETY

- Although lead-free enamels are available, many do contain lead. Take care, when using small paintbrushes or a goose quill with enamels, not to lick the ends, as they will contain small particles of lead.
- Take care when using a kiln for enameling. Place the kiln on a steel or ceramic surface and wear insulated gloves when inserting or removing items from it.

ENAMELING METHODS

SIFTED ENAMEL: the enamel is washed, dried, and sifted through a fine sifter directly onto the metal. It can be fired immediately. This method is used initially when the area to be enameled is larger than $2^1/_2$ inches/6cm square. It is very often used on copper work, and is useful when applying a base coat of flux to silver.

WET PACK ENAMEL: wet enamel is laid onto the metal and spread out thinly to give a fine, even layer. It must dry completely before being fired. This is the usual way of applying enamel to silver or gold for jewelry.

RONDE BOSSE: wet enamel is applied to a three-dimensional surface. To hold the enamel in place, the surface is painted with gum tragacanth or enamel glue. The water is drawn off the enamel with a cloth or paper towel at regular intervals to stop it sliding around.

CHAMPLEVÉ: enamel is laid into an area that has either been etched away or removed by hand engraving. It is fired in thin, even layers until it reaches the level of the surrounding metal. The name comes from the French, *champ levé*, meaning "raised field."

CLOISONNÉ: enamel is placed into small cells made with very fine wire that has been drawn down flat and cut to form the pattern required. The wires are either placed on edge onto a basecoat enamel and fired in, or placed on edge into the etched-out area and soldered in. In order to stand upright and on edge, each cloisonné wire needs to have a curve or slightly angled area, which can be included as part of the design.

BASSE TAILLE: transparent enamel is placed over a low or deep cut which has been made in the metal before the application of the enamel. The pattern and shapes carved beneath the enamel show through and the different depths in the enamel produce different depths of color.

PLIQUÉ À JOUR, OR WINDOW ENAMELING: the enamel has no metal background. When a finished piece is held up to the light, it has the appearance of a stained glass window. Usually a pattern is pierced out of the metal and the wet enamel is held in the pierced-out areas by capillary action. It must be completely dry before firing. To assist with holding the enamel in, a background sheet of "Mica" can be used.

PAINTED ENAMEL: a light, opaque enamel is fired onto metal and smoothed down with a carborundum stone and wet-and-dry papers. Painting enamels differ from other enamels in that they are ground extremely finely and mixed with a pure oil medium before being painted onto an opaque enamel surface. They must dry for at least an hour before firing.

GRISAILLE: layers of white enamel following a pattern or picture are fired on top of black enamel basecoat to give a gradual, shaded effect.

SGRAFFITO: lines are drawn through the enamel once it has dried. The piece is then fired and either the color underneath the line is exposed, or another color is placed in the line and fired.

MILLEFIORE AND STICKS: these are manufactured shapes of enamel that can be added onto a coat of enamel and fired in.

ENAMEL PREPARATION

Enamel is supplied in either lump or powdered form. The lumps must be ground before use, and both forms must be washed. Opaque and transparent enamels are prepared in the same way.

❶ Place the quantity of lump enamel required into a mortar. To provide three or four coats over an area of 1 inch/ 2cm square, approximately 4-5g are required. Half-fill the mortar with filtered water. Use a pestle to break up the lumps, or a mallet to hit the top of the pestle to help further break it up. Grind in a circular movement for a few minutes until it is really fine and making a "smooth" sound.

The water will be cloudy as you start to grind and wash the enamel.

❷ After grinding down to the fineness required, tap the side of the mortar with the pestle to settle the enamel. Pour off the water and replace with fresh. Swirl water around in the bowl to wash the enamel and then pour it off again. Repeat until the water is completely clear.

❸ Remove the enamel from the mortar and place in a palette or a small, plastic, container with a screw-top lid. Keep covered with water and sealed until ready to use. Wet enamels can be kept in this way for a month. They may need to be washed again before subsequent use.

After the final rinsing, the water should be completely clear.

DRY ENAMEL (FOR SIFTING)

After washing and grinding, leave the enamel in the mortar and put on top of a warm kiln to dry. Use it fairly quickly as it will deteriorate if kept in a container for too long.

METAL PREPARATION

Enamel will adhere only to perfectly clean metal.

❶ Anneal, pickle, and rinse the metal, and then place in a hot solution of baking soda to ensure that there is no trace of remaining pickle. Scrub it with a soft brush with a little liquid detergent or a glass brush. When the metal is really clean, water will stay on the whole surface and not form globules. If water pulls away from any area of the metal, so will the enamel.

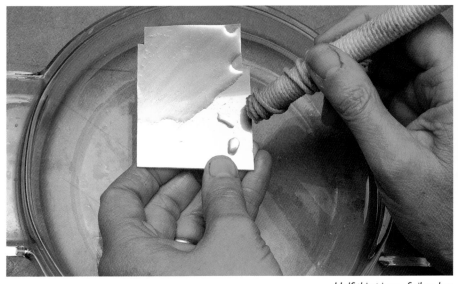

Half this piece of silver has been cleaned with a glass brush. The area with the globules is still greasy.

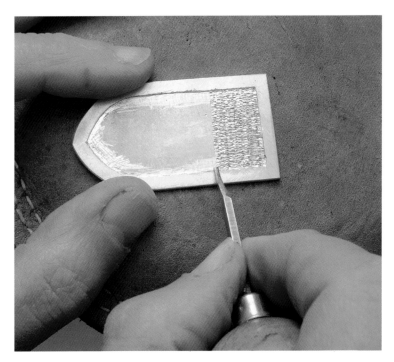

❷ If any soldering has to be done before enameling, do it with hard or enameling solder. Anneal and pickle the piece at least three times to provide a good base for the enamel.

❸ To produce a highly-reflective effect under enamel, cut a piece by hand, very evenly, with a small cutting tool, and then clean in the same way. Do any cutting to produce the basse taille effect before final cleaning.

❹ Keep the metal under water until everything is prepared for enamel application.

Use a small cutter to make an overall pattern before enameling.

APPLICATION AND FIRING

Make sure that the metal to which the enamel is to be applied is dry. When enameling on silver, it is usual for the first coat of enamel to be a "flux" enamel. This prevents any firescale from appearing under the enamels and making them appear dull and cloudy. Flux can also be used as a first coat for copper, when the effects of firescale under the enamel are often rather interesting and worth a little experimentation.

Keep the temperature of the kiln for enameling around 1,652°F/900°C. At this temperature the inside of the kiln will be bright red.

❶ Heat a kiln to 1,652°F/900°C. The enamels should be in front of you, kept under water, in a palette or plastic container.

❷ With a goose quill or metal spatula, pull some of the enamel out from the water and spread it evenly onto the metal. If there is too much water to prevent the enamel from spreading evenly, draw it away with the corner of a paper towel. Continue until the enamel has covered the whole area and then allow it to dry completely before firing.

The wet enamel is laid onto the silver with the sharpened end of a goose quill.

❸ Place the enamel on wire mesh and, using a long fork, hold it at the mouth of the open kiln for a few seconds to ensure it is dry. Close the door of the kiln, to allow it to regain the correct temperature before placing the enamel inside.

❹ The length of time required to fire the enamel varies, depending on the size of the piece, the type and thickness of the metal, and which enamels are being used. An average-sized piece, 1 inch/3cm² x $^1/_{16}$ inch/1mm thick, would require a firing time of 50 to 60 seconds, but check every 15 seconds and remove it when the enamel begins to look shiny.

❺ Remove the enamel from the kiln, and allow it to cool before applying the next coat. Repeat the firing, and continue this process until either the enamel is just slightly higher than the surrounding metal (champlevé) or the required depth of color has been reached (en bosse ronde, basse taille). The enamel is now ready to be stoned down

STONE DOWN THE ENAMEL

❶ To achieve a smooth and even surface to the enamel, use a carborundum stone, coarse wet-and-dry paper (220-grade), or a diamond grit strip. Hold the piece under running water and hold the stone, or alternatives, horizontally across the work to rub it down until it is smooth. Finish with finer wet-and-dry papers, either 400- or 600-grades.

❷ Allow the piece to dry completely, and then re-fire for a final time to reveal the true color and shine.

Hold the enamel flat so that the rubbing down is smooth.

SAMPLES • **Enameling**

Enameling adds a completely new dimension to a piece. You can get some brilliant results by playing with all the different colors on copper, but be prepared to take more time and care to get really good results on silver. Although a gas- or electric-fired kiln is essential for enameling on silver, most enamels on copper can be fired with a normal soldering torch. The samples here vary from a piece prepared in minutes, to a piece taking several hours.

HOW THE SAMPLES WERE ACHIEVED

SUBSTRATE 1-6

COPPER

❶ Hard white enamel was sifted on to the metal and fired. Small transparent and opaque lumps of enamel were placed on the white base and fired.

❷ Hard white enamel was sifted onto the metal and fired. A metal stencil was held on the work and green enamel was sifted through it. The stencil was then removed and the piece fired.

❸ Sgraffito effect achieved by a hard transparent flux fired as a base coat. Wet red and black enamel were laid on top of the flux coat. When the black was dry, a line was drawn with a sharp point. The enamel was then fired. Fine silver filings were sprinkled on the surface and the piece was fired again.

❹ A hard white enamel base coat was stoned down after firing. Black lines were then painted on and fired. The colored painting enamels were ground with lavender oil and painted on and left to dry for one hour before firing.

❺ A base coat of hard transparent flux was fired. Red transparent enamel was placed in zigzag lines and a blue flux placed between. The piece was refired before black lines and dots were painted on and it was fired once more.

❻ Following preparation as in sample 5, cloisonné wires were placed onto the fired flux and the piece was refired. The colored enamels were placed into and around the cloisons and fired. Three further firings were required to fill up the cloisons. The piece was stoned down and refired.

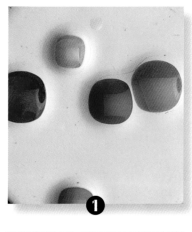

❶

❷

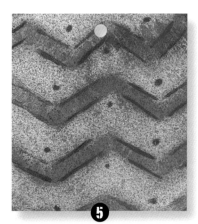

❸

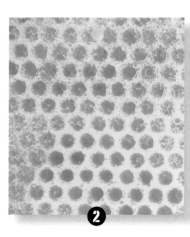

❹

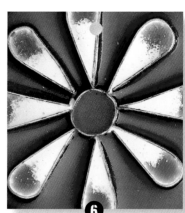

❺

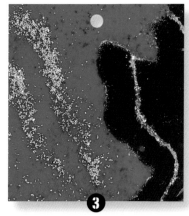

❻

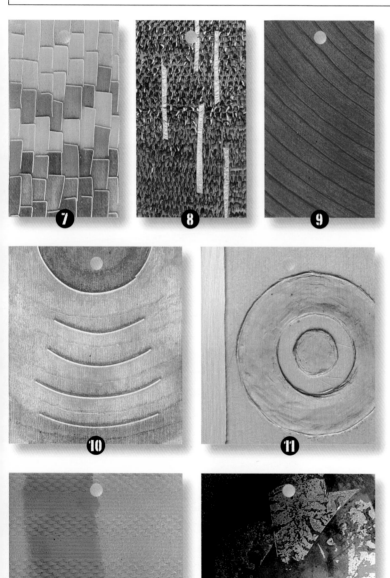

SUBSTRATE 7-11

PHOTOETCHED SILVER

7 A base coat of blue flux was fired. The fine silver cloisonné wires were placed on top of the flux and fired. Colored enamels were laid wet into the cloisons and fired when dry. When the cloisons were full, the piece was stoned down and refired.

8 The background was cut with a graver. Purple transparent enamel was laid directly onto the silver and fired. Silver foil was laid in strips on top of the enamel and the piece fired again.

9 For this basse taille effect, the lines were hand-engraved into the silver base. Blue transparent enamel was laid wet into the etched area. The depth of the engraved lines affects the brightness or darkness of the blue color.

10 A base coat of blue flux was fired. Cloisonné wires were laid on top and fired in. Colors were applied and when the enamel was full it was stoned down and refired. Stop-out fluid was painted onto the whole piece, except in the areas to be etched. The piece was placed in hydrofluoric acid for 1 hour to etch lines in the enamel. The stop-out was removed.

11 The pattern was hand-engraved using the basse taille method. Gray transparent enamel was used to give a "glassy" look.

SUBSTRATE 12-13

SILVER

12 Different blues were laid either directly onto a machine-engraved background or over a flux base coat for a color test.

13 For this ronde bosse effect, the enamel was fired on to a metal dome. Several layers of transparent and opaque enamels were applied. Silver foil was added on the last firing and rubbed gently afterward with fine steel wool.

SHOWCASE • **Enameling**

This showcase displays just a few of the huge range of enameling effects. In some of these pieces, enamel is used as a highlight, set into the work in place of a stone; for other pieces it is the *raison d'être*. Enamel can be as colorful or as subtle as you like. The gray target pendant exudes cool and calm, while the pink necklace simply demands attention!

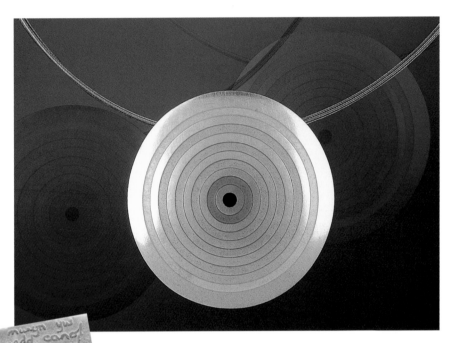

GRAY TARGET PENDANT

Jane Moore • Sterling silver and enamel
Enamel in photoetched concentric circles on a silver disc forms a simple pendant.

PINK NECKLACE

Jinks McGrath • Sterling silver, 24-carat gold, enamel, and rubies
This beautiful silver necklace has been made up of individual discs, some of which have cloisonné enamel. Others have been set with cabochon rubies or textured with fused gold.

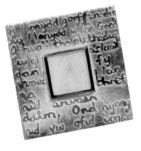

EIFIONYDD COLLECTION

Mari Thomas and Emma Sedman
• Sterling silver and enamel
Enamel provides a strong, colorful focal point for these pieces.

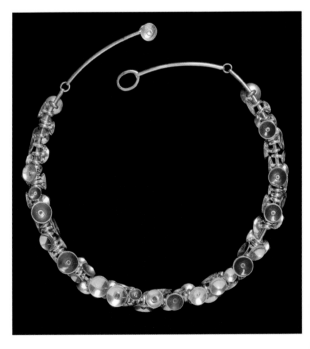

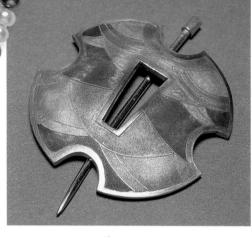

PEARL LOCKET

Jinks McGrath • Sterling silver and 24-carat gold
The body of this locket has been made with fused 24-carat gold onto textured silver. The front piece is enamel with fused gold in an interpretation of Indian fabric design.

CLOISONNÉ BROOCH

Kyoko Urino • Silver on enamel
Cloisonné enameling with subtle colors has been applied over a ground of traditional Japanese wave patterns. The form of the brooch has been inspired by the tuba, a Japanese sword.

EIFIONYDD COLLECTION

Mari Thomas and Emma Sedman • Sterling silver and enamel
This collection of jewelry uses transparent enamel over a textured surface to create a contrast to the etched text of the pieces.

CORDED PENDANT

Kyoko Urino • Silver with enamel and silk cord
This pendant has been formed from a domed disc with two crescents pierced out, one for the silk cord, one for champlevé enamel. Pliqué à jour enamel has also been used for decoration. The color of the enamel and silk cord complement each other and contrast with the patination that has been used on the main body of the piece.

TECHNIQUE • Engraving

Hand engraving requires time, practice, and patience. It is an exceptionally skillful technique—the best work is by those who have spent years at their craft. However, it is well worth learning the rudiments of engraving skills in order to enhance a plain surface. Engraving effects can also be achieved by using an electric tool, known as a pendant motor. This has different burrs and diamond-tipped tools to create all kinds of different effects.

Keep hand-engraving tools properly sharpened; the best tool for this is a fine carborundum or Arkansas stone. Gravers are sold without handles so that the length can be adjusted to fit individual needs. The electric pendant motor is usually conveniently positioned just above the jewelry workbench, ready for use.

PENDANT MOTORS

There are various types of workbench-based pendant motors to which different burrs and cutters can be fitted. Diamond burrs are supplied either as a cone, disc, round, or parallel-shaped, and are sharp enough to give a good cut into areas required. "Ball-shaped" cutters in fine, medium, and coarse grades make a round, hollowing cut. Less aggressive burrs will simply mark smooth linear patterns or crosshatching.

The pendant motor is also an excellent tool for cleaning and polishing small areas. Wet-and-dry paper can be fixed into a split spindle to smooth the inner side of rings. Fine silicon rubber points, in a variety of shapes, will give a clean satin finish to metal, and there are others made especially to give a great shine on platinum. Small felt brushes and mops are used with the same polishes as are used on large polishing motors.

PENDANT MOTOR
① *Handle*
② *Tools*
③ *Pendant motor*

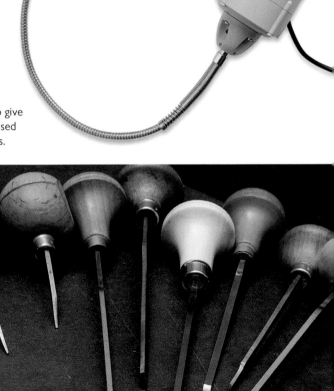

HAND ENGRAVERS
A selection of gravers with different shaped ends.

SAFETY

- The tips of gravers are very sharp. Always keep them in their container or with a guard, such as a cork, over the tips.
- Hold the article to be engraved either in a hand-held engraver's vise or on a leather-covered sandbag.
- Tuck the handle of the tool comfortably inside the palm of the hand, while holding the graver between the thumb and first finger. Hold the article being engraved with the other hand, placing the first finger in front of the thumb of the tool hand, to act as a brake. This prevents the graver from sliding out of control and also ensures that, as the graver cuts along the metal, there are no fingers from the supporting hand in the way. The thumb of the tool hand controls all the work done with the graver.

The handle of the graver should sit comfortably in the palm of the hand so that there is not too long an end protruding.

TRANSFERRING A PATTERN TO METAL

Keep metal sheet clean and free from scratches before the pattern to be engraved is transferred onto the metal. Prepare the metal using wet-and-dry papers from 220 through to 1200 to achieve a fine finish (see Polished, Matt, and Satin Finishes, page 34).

Trace the pattern onto a piece of tracing paper. Turn over the tracing paper, and with a soft pencil scribble over the lines of the pattern. Place the tracing paper, pattern upward, over the metal sheet and secure. Use a scribe to follow the lines of the pattern to transfer them onto the metal. Remove the tracing paper and go over the transferred carbon lines with a scribe. Keep the lines thin but firm. It is impossible to follow a feathery line!

SHARPENING GRAVERS

Keep engraving tools as sharp as possible. The sharper they are, the easier the cutting will be. Shape a new tool initially on a carborundum wheel, but finish it by hand on a fine carborundum wheel or Arkansas stone. Keep the stone within easy reach on the bench and keep it oiled.

❶ Hold the handle of the tool in the palm of the hand and hold the graver tip flat on the stone at the angle to which it has been cut. The face should be absolutely flat across the stone. Rub it up and around the stone, keeping it at exactly the same angle all the time.

❷ When the tip is sharp, lay the graver with its underside just higher than flat on the stone and rub lightly on it to remove any build up of metal on the underside of the tip. The test of a sharp graver is to try it against a thumbnail: It should just start to hold into it. A number of gravers have an angle ground away from the underside. This is to make sure that the underside does not mark the metal as the topside is doing the cutting.

Hold the face of the graver so that it is completely flat on the sharpening stone.

ENGRAVING A STRAIGHT LINE

Use the lozenge-shaped graver for a straight line.

To begin the line, hold the tip on the line and raise the handle about 70 degrees above the metal sheet to allow the point to just feel the start of the line. Lower the handle to about 20 degrees and push the graver along the line for a short distance. As the stroke is finished, the point of the graver is flicked upward. Do not try to engrave too long a line as the point may slip and make a scratch.

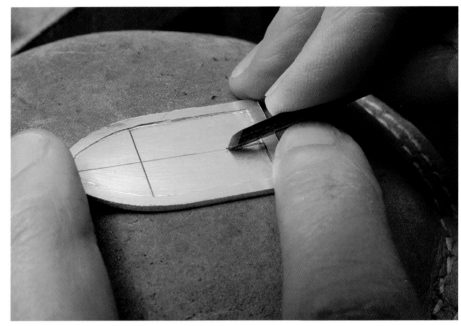

Flick away shards of silver at frequent intervals when cutting a straight line with a lozenge-shaped graver.

ENGRAVING A CURVED LINE

Use the lozenge-shaped graver for a curved line.

Position the piece so that it can be turned as the line is engraved. The main rule is that the body and handle of the tool should follow the direction of the point. Cut a curved line toward rather than away from you. The curve can be emphasized by slightly rolling the graver as it follows the line to either the left or the right. It is wise to take small cuts at a time, until one becomes more practiced and skilled.

Lean the lozenge-shaped cutter into the bend as it is being cut.

ENGRAVED FEATHER
Liz Olver
The subtle, almost natural engraved detailing on this pendant transforms a simple form into a delicate work of art.

ENGRAVING OUT AN AREA
Use the lozenge-shaped and square-ended gravers together with a spitstick.

Cut a line just inside the finish line with a lozenge-shaped graver. Using a square-ended graver, broaden the line to remove all the metal required. To keep the newly-exposed surface level, use the graver at a very shallow angle. Then trim up the edges to the outside line with a spitstick.

Use a cutter with a broader end to remove the metal from a larger area.

LILY OF THE VALLEY BROOCH
Margaret Shepherd
Engraved 20-carat red gold leaves sit on a pierced 18-carat yellow gold base. The piece is ornamented with rubies and lilies of the valley in white gold.

Whether engraving by hand or using a pendant motor, you will be able to achieve an enormous variety of finishes. As these samples show, engraving is not simply about creating lines or shapes; it can also be used to produce an overall effect as well as a background for enameling. Engraved lines can be emphasized with oxidization. Cross-hatching can be used to create a shadow effect.

HOW THE SAMPLES WERE ACHIEVED

SUBSTRATE 1-3

BRASS

❶ A circle was marked with a scribe and the interior engraved with a small round cutting tool, the "frazier" on a pendant motor. Outer lines were made with a tapered diamond burr on a pendant motor.

❷ Effect achieved using a silicone rubber wheel on a pendant motor.

❸ Kite pattern produced using a "mounted grindstone" on the pendant motor.

SUBSTRATE 4-8

SILVER

❹ The sketch was drawn with a scribe and a lozenge hand graver used to engrave out the pattern. It was oxidized and the surface cleaned with fine wet-and-dry paper to darken the engraved lines.

❺ Flower pattern sketched with a soft pencil, and engraved with a lozenge graver.

❻ Piece formed in a fly press. The outer and inner lines were marked with a soft pencil and then engraved with, first a lozenge and then a small flat edge graver. The inside was marked with a "shading tool," a graver with multi lines.

❼ Triangles marked using a template and scribe. The top triangle was marked with a round-edge graver, the center triangle with a lozenge graver, and the lowest triangle with a knife-edge graver.

❽ Leaf pattern showing different line thicknesses. The outline was engraved with a lozenge graver and then a flat-edge graver, while the inner lines were engraved using a round-edge tool.

HELPFUL HINTS

- Keep hand-engraving tools sharp. The tips will stay sharper if stored with a cork on their ends.
- If you slip with a hand-engraver and make an unplanned line, rub over it with a burnisher before using wet-and-dry paper.
- Hold work to be engraved either on a sand bag or in a special engraving holder.
- If you are using a pendant motor to engrave, always try out the tool on a piece of scrap metal first.
- Lightly draw the lines to be engraved on the surface with a scribe. A pencil line will always rub off.
- Make sure the engraved line is deep enough not to disappear when the piece is rubbed down or polished.

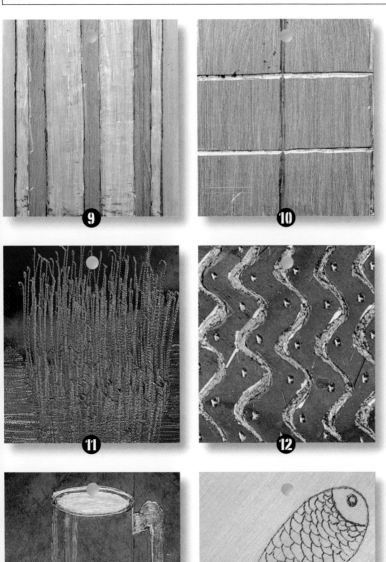

SUBSTRATE 9-10

SILVER

9 Engraving showing different depths cut for the enameling on top. The lines were engraved with a lozenge graver, and then with a small flat-edge tool, finishing with a "chisel" engraving tool.

10 Lines cut for future enameling using a lozenge graver. The surface was cleaned with fine wet-and-dry paper.

SUBSTRATE 11-14

COPPER

11 Sketchy engraving done with a tapered diamond burr applied in different directions. The burr was held in a pendant motor.

12 Pattern outlined with a scribe, and engraved using a parallel diamond burr and a small round-headed diamond burr.

13 Tankard design marked with a soft pencil and then engraved with a lozenge graver. The shading was done with a multi-lined "shading tool."

14 Fish pattern sketched with a soft pencil. A fine tapered diamond burr was used on a pendant motor to engrave the detail. It was finished with fine wet-and-dry paper.

SHOWCASE • **Engraving**

The designs in this showcase demonstrate the use of engraving either as an incidental effect, or as the main feature of a piece. The lily of the valley armband and the tiger moth brooch both use engraving to highlight certain areas, while for the earrings *(below right)*, the technique is integral to the design.

TIGER MOTH BROOCH
Margaret Shepherd •
Sterling silver, 22- and
18-carat gold
Engraving has been used as part of this piece to add realism to the moth forms. The 22-carat gold on the wings of the larger moth has an engraved texture to enhance the level of detail on the piece as a whole.

LILY OF THE VALLEY ARMBAND
Margaret Shepherd • 18-carat yellow, white, and red gold
The engraved lines on the leaves of the stylized design add realism and contrast to a sumptuous bangle.

PRICE TAG BRACELET
Stacey Lorinczi • Silver and 23-carat vermeil
This bracelet makes a statement about consumer culture with its price tag charms engraved with prices in different currencies—American dollars, British pounds, Japanese yen, old French francs, and Portuguese escudos.

EARRINGS
Harriet St Leger • Gold and pearls
The lacelike effect on these earrings has been created using a pendant motor burr to engrave the surface of the gold.

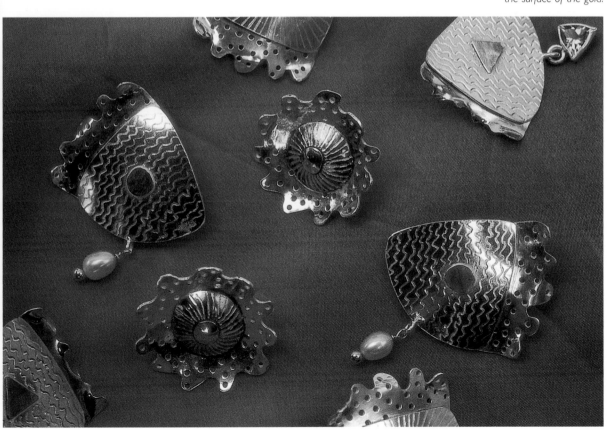

TECHNIQUE • **Inlay**

Inlay is the term used to describe the surface of a metal that has distinct areas of contrasting metals laid into it as a pattern or an outline. The magnificent Taj Mahal in Agra, India, is the most inspiring example of inlay. Carnelian, agates, and nephrite jade are inlaid into white marble to form floral patterns on both the inside and outside of the mausoleum. Other examples of inlay are wooden boxes made in the East, inlaid with fine brass, copper, and silver wires, or cut-out sheets of marble or stone, to form charming patterns and pictures.

There are several ways of achieving a similar end. The traditional method cuts channels into metal using chisels, and then hammers wires of contrasting metals into the channels. Easier methods include, instead of the use of wires, running solder into grooves that have been engraved out of the metal. Another is to pierce a shape out of a thin metal and solder a thicker, contrasting piece behind it and run it through a rolling mill. Yet another is to pierce a shape out of one metal and cut the identical shape into another and solder the shape into it.

INLAY EQUIPMENT
① *Chisels with different-sized heads for cutting channels*
② *Steel stock (for making chisels)*

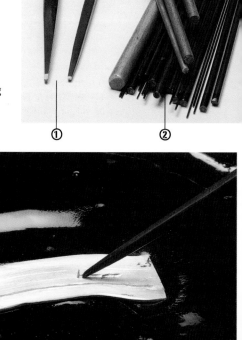

①   ②

TRADITIONAL METHOD

Traditional inlay uses different-sized chisels, which are hit directly with a chasing hammer. Hold the work in an engraver's ball vise (to make turning easy) or in a pitch bowl. Mark the pattern to be followed on the work with a scribe before holding it down.

❶ Hold the chisel at 90 degrees to the work and hit it with the hammer to get the cut going. Tilt at the angle shown (see right) and work along the line at the required depth. As the metal curves up, remove it to keep the line clear. Continue until the line is completed or the outline for a larger area has been cut.

❷ Remove the metal inside the pattern using a wider chisel and then use a graver to level the floor of the cut-out area.

❸ Inlay round wire into a single groove or cut sheet metal to fit into a larger cut-out area.

Use a steel chisel to cut out the channel for wire. Keep the chisel sharp so that the silver is cut cleanly.

TO INLAY ROUND WIRE:

Use wire of the same diameter as the cut groove. Push one end of the wire into the groove and use a hammer or matting tool to push the wire into the groove. The edges will have been slightly raised by the action of the chisel and can be pushed down over the inlaid wire to hold them in.

After fixing the end of the wire into the start of the chiseled groove, hammer it down.

TO INLAY SHEET METAL INTO A CUT-OUT:

Anneal, pickle, and clean the piece to be inlaid. Shape it slightly concave and place it over the cut-out area of the base. Using a wooden mallet, gently hammer it into position and close over the raised edge of the outline to secure the shape into the metal.

Use a matting tool to push down the sides of the silver channel, which were slightly raised by the cut of the chisel.

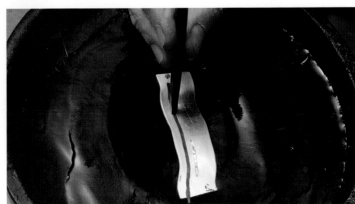

SOLDER METHOD

Solder inlay requires a groove to be channeled in the metal just deep enough to take solder. This can be stamped in with a punch, engraved using a graver, or by using a chasing tool as described in *Chasing and Repoussé* (see page 118). Other possibilities include making an indent into the metal with wire through a rolling mill or by etching a shallow line.

❶ Flux inside the recessed lines. Place tiny paillons of contrasting solder at close intervals along the lines. Heat the work slowly so that the paillons do not blow away or move, and gradually increase the heat until the solder starts to flow into the lines.

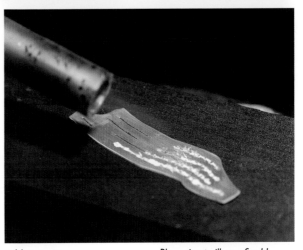

❷ Alternatively, use stick soldering to fill the lines. Cut pieces of solder in lengths of $1^1/_2$ x $1/_{16}$ inch/40mm x 1mm and paint flux on them. Line them up so that they can be picked up quickly one after another. Place a small paillon of solder at the beginning of a line and heat up the work until the solder starts to flow. Holding the solder stick in insulated tweezers, introduce the tip of the solder to the line and move it up the line as it flows. Continue until all the lines are filled.

❸ Both these methods will produce solder overspills. Remove these by filing and then working the whole piece smooth with wet-and-dry papers.

❹ To impress a pattern on the piece, put it through a rolling mill with a patterned paper or cloth.

Place tiny paillons of gold together along the line and solder in. This gives a contrasting color.

INLAYING CONTRASTING METALS (SWEAT SOLDERING)

Pierce a pattern out in a sheet of metal of no more than 0.5mm thickness. The end result will not be precise, as it becomes distorted when passed through a rolling mill, so design the piece accordingly.

❶ Paint the back of the pierced piece with flux. Evenly distribute small paillons of solder on top of the flux. Heat, and allow each of the solder paillons to run into a flattish "blob."

❷ Pickle and clean the piece, and file off the top of the blob with a flat file but leave the solder clearly visible. Re-flux it and place it on top of a contrasting piece of metal approximately $^1/_{16}$ inch/1mm thick, so that the different color shows through the pattern. The two pieces of metal should sit flat together. Tie them together with binding wire before soldering.

❸ Place a paillon of the same solder at the edge and heat it up until the solder starts to flow. Maintain the heat to allow the solder in the middle to flow and join the two pieces.

❹ Pickle the piece and rinse in water. Boil in a solution of 1 tablespoon baking soda to 1 cup (250ml) water, and then give a final rinse in water. Dry it thoroughly and then roll it through a rolling mill until the metal at the back has been pushed through the pierced area and is flat. As the piece is rolled out, the orientation should be changed with each pass.

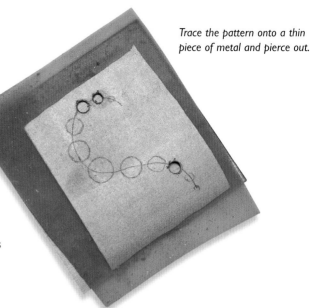

Trace the pattern onto a thin piece of metal and pierce out.

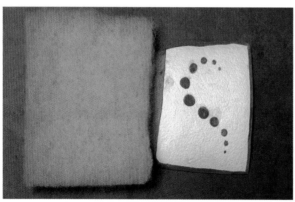

These soldered pieces of silver and copper were passed through a rolling mill several times to push the copper up through the pierced-out pattern. The final rolling was done with some cotton fabric to give an interesting finish to the surface.

PIERCING OUT AND FITTING IN

This method of inlay needs to be very accurate. It works well with large cut-out areas and it is easier if the metal used is no thicker than $^1/_{16}$ inch/1mm.

❶ Pierce out the pattern in the first sheet of metal. Clean and file to exactly the shape required. Place double-sided sticky tape on the back of the pattern and press it down onto a second sheet of metal.

❷ Use a fine scribe to trace round the edge of the pattern. The more accurate the line at this stage, the easier the subsequent soldering will be.

❸ Drill a 0.5mm hole inside the line and thread the piercing saw blade through it. Pierce out the area by keeping to the inside of the line.

Cut out the white gold piece to be inlaid first. Then cut out the area of yellow gold that it will fit into inside the line. File to fit.

4 Flux the edges of both pieces, place solder across the back of both, and solder. Ensure the inlay fits exactly before soldering. If there are any gaps between the inlay and the outer piece, soldering will make them larger as it draws in the edges in areas that are a good fit.

Solder the white gold interior and yellow gold surround together and dome. Use easy solder to join on a backing piece.

Place tiny paillons of solder around the base of the white gold inlaid piece to solder it into the yellow gold base.

STRIP EARRINGS
Jill Newbrook
The sheer, subtle, minimalist effect of these bands of inlaid silver and 18-carat white gold is given a twist with some ruby studs.

DANDELION CLOCK BROOCH
Margaret Shepherd
This silver dandelion "clock" brooch, with its hanging silver stem, is inlaid with shakudo, shibuchi, and 18-carat gold.

SAMPLES • **Inlay**

The intention with inlay is to produce a flat surface of contrasting metals. The resulting beautifully subtle change of color is difficult to achieve in any other way. A variety of materials from very fine wires to intricately pierced sheet metal can be inlaid into another metal. The finished effect should look as if it is all one piece.

HOW THE SAMPLES WERE ACHIEVED

SUBSTRATE 1-3

SILVER

❶ The swirl was cut from textured silver, and its outline traced with a pin onto plain sheet silver. The receiving area was pierced out, and the swirl pushed in and soldered from the back.

❷ Circles, decreasing in size, were pierced out of 0.5mm sheet silver. Hard solder was run on the back of the silver and the high areas filed flat. The silver was soldered to 1mm thick copper sheet and put through a rolling mill until the copper was level with the silver. It was annealed and passed again through a rolling mill with a texturizing cotton.

❸ The shape was cut from silver, annealed, and hammered with a ball-pein hammer. Lines were engraved with a lozenge graver and 0.5mm gold wire was soldered into them with silver solder. The wire was flattened with a jeweler's hammer.

SUBSTRATE 4

GOLD

❹ The center shapes were cut from 18-carat 0.5mm white gold sheet. The same shape was cut out of 18-carat red 0.5mm gold sheet. The pieces were pushed into each other, soldered in with yellow gold solder, and domed before being cleaned with wet-and-dry papers. They are shown here prior to final finishing for earstuds.

SUBSTRATE 5

COPPER

❺ The main piece of copper was pierced with a crisscross pattern. Solder was run on the back of the metal and it was soldered to the brass back piece. The whole piece was rolled through a mill until the brass was level with the copper.

❶

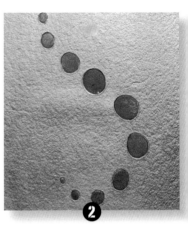
❷

❸

❹

❺

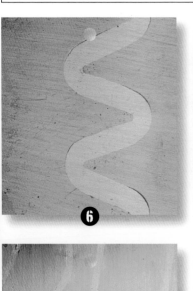

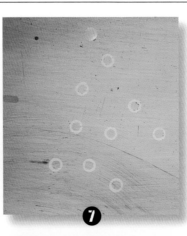

SUBSTRATE 6-7

COPPER

6 The shape was formed with 1mm diameter silver wire and the bottom filed flat. It was soldered to the base metal and passed through the rolling mill until the shape reached the level of the back piece.

7 A center punch was used to mark the position of the inlay on the copper, and 1mm diameter holes were drilled. Lengths of 1mm diameter silver chenier (tubing) were pushed into the holes and soldered in. Smaller diameter copper wire was placed inside each inlaid piece and soldered in. The ends of both the chenier and copper wire were pierced and filed away.

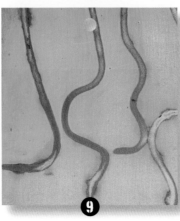

SUBSTRATE 8-10

BRASS

8 A lozenge graver was used to engrave the pattern. Fine silver wire was hammered into the engraved areas and soldered in.

9 The pattern was engraved using a lozenge graver. Tiny paillons of silver solder were laid into the engraved lines at close intervals. The piece was heated until the solder flowed and filled the lines. It was finished with a progression of wet-and-dry papers from 220 to 1200, and then oxidized in a potassium sulfate solution. The silver solder oxidizes, but the brass does not.

10 A diamond shape was cut out of brass. A fractionally smaller diamond shape was cut in copper and filed for an exact fit. The brass was soldered in from the back. After cleaning with wet-and-dry papers from 220 to 600, the piece was oxidized. The copper oxidizes, but the brass does not.

SHOWCASE • **Inlay**

From fine and subtle to bold and figurative, inlay can take you in many different directions. The essence of this technique is that, no matter how many patterns and colors are used, the surface is leveled to allow light to reflect off a piece undisturbed.

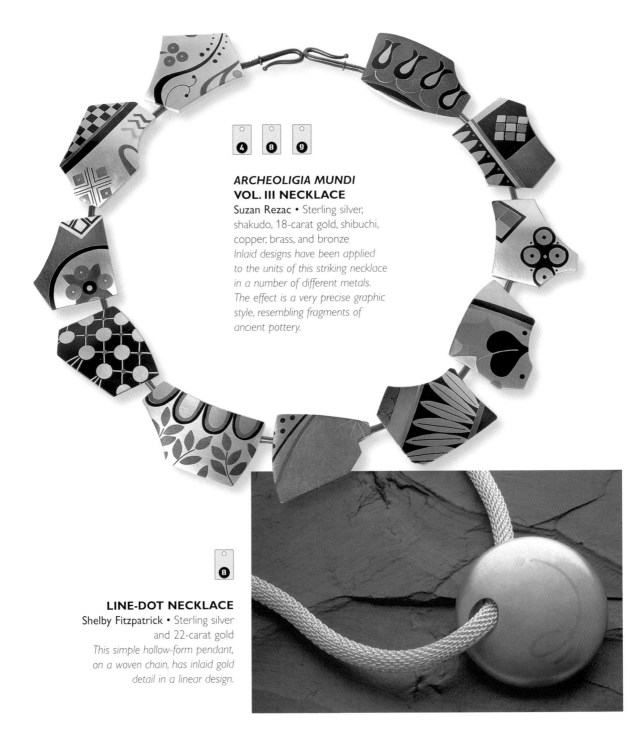

ARCHEOLIGIA MUNDI VOL. III NECKLACE

Suzan Rezac • Sterling silver, shakudo, 18-carat gold, shibuchi, copper, brass, and bronze
Inlaid designs have been applied to the units of this striking necklace in a number of different metals. The effect is a very precise graphic style, resembling fragments of ancient pottery.

LINE-DOT NECKLACE

Shelby Fitzpatrick • Sterling silver and 22-carat gold
This simple hollow-form pendant, on a woven chain, has inlaid gold detail in a linear design.

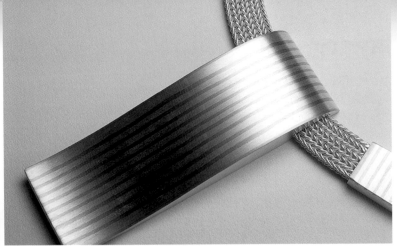

PALLADIUM PENDANT AND EARRINGS

Jill Newbrook • Sterling silver, palladium, and 22-carat yellow gold
The clean lines of this piece have been emphasized with the use of palladium inlaid in bands across the silver, and framed with yellow gold. The subtle variations in the color of the metal are particularly effective. The stylish earrings have been suspended from black pearls for a slick color combination.

FEATHER EARRINGS

Margaret Shepherd •
Sterling silver, 18-carat gold, and rubies
The bands of gold inlay on these elegant earrings contrast with the oxidization to create the impression of an exotic feather.

DOUBLE MUSICAL RINGS

Shelby Fitzpatrick • Sterling silver and gold
This set of chiming rings, displayed here as pendants, use gold detail on silver forms to create a bold pattern in subtle colors.

TECHNIQUE • **Chasing and repoussé**

These two decorative techniques are used in conjunction with each other and are usually applied to three-dimensional forms such as fish, water, birds, animals, and plants to create patterns, shapes, and lines. Chasing is done on the front of the work while repoussé is worked from the back. The technique uses "pitch", which is a mixture of bitumen, plaster, and wax. Keep pitch in a heavy metal bowl set in a wooden ring.

CHASING AND REPOUSSÉ EQUIPMENT
① *Repoussé punches*
② *Chasing hammer*
③ *Bowl of hot pitch*

Chasing tools are fine instruments that will spread and delineate a line onto a metal surface, or make a pattern of small lines, dots, cross-hatching, or curves. A small, flat-sided hammer is used to achieve a rhythmical and continuous tapping of the chasing tools across the work.

Repoussé tools are punches with smooth sides. Shapes are worked from the back by gradually hammering the punches into the area that will be raised when seen from the front. A ball-pein hammer is used with the punches.

① ② ③

SAFETY
• Use hot pitch with great care, as it can give a painful burn. When burning pitch off a piece of metal to clean it, always hold the work over the pitch bowl to allow any drips to fall into the bowl and not onto your hands.
• If you need to touch the pitch to help it hold over metal, dip your fingers in cold water first.
• Take care with sharp chasing tools. Use the little finger as a brake on the metal to stop the punch slipping forward.

If you dip your finger into cold water first, you will be able to safely push the pitch over the metal to hold it in firmly.

TRANSFERRING THE PATTERN

Anneal the metal and give it a soft matt surface using some fine wet-and-dry paper. A pattern or picture can then be transferred onto the surface of the metal, using either of these two methods:

Method 1: Trace the pattern onto tracing paper. On the reverse side, cover all the lines of the pattern with a soft pencil. Tape the tracing paper, reverse side down, onto the metal. With a scribe, follow all the lines of the pattern to transfer the carbon marks onto the surface of the metal. Remove the paper and use the scribe again to outline a firmer line around the pattern. Go to Chasing the Outline (right).

Use a scribe to transfer a pencil line through the tracing paper and onto the metal.

Method 2: Alternatively, fold a piece of tracing paper in half and slip the piece of metal inside it. Mark the pattern onto the tracing paper so that it sits over the central area of the metal. Remove the metal and trace the pattern onto the folded back piece of tracing paper. On the reverse of each side of the paper, cover all the lines of the pattern using a soft pencil. Tape the paper around the metal. With a scribe, follow the lines of the pattern on both sides to transfer the carbon marks onto the metal. Remove the paper and use the scribe again to draw firmer lines on both sides of the metal. Go to Chasing the Outline (right).

CHASING THE OUTLINE

❶ Bend down each corner of the top side of the annealed metal with flat-nosed pliers. Heat the pitch with a gentle flame and place the metal into it topside up. Push the softened pitch over the edges of the metal to secure it in place. Allow to cool.

❷ Chase the outline of the pattern into the metal with a tracer punch, which has a slightly smooth, chisel-shaped head. Hold it between the thumb and three fingers at an angle where the top is away from you and the bottom coming toward you. This angle makes it easy to see the line that is being chased.

❸ Once the pattern has been chased onto the metal, gently heat it again until it can be lifted from the pitch and annealed. Any remaining pitch will burn away as the metal is annealed. The bends in the corners are then reversed and the metal replaced in the pitch underside up.

❹ Press the shapes required in the metal down into the pitch using the repoussé punches. If the metal is well annealed, quite deep impressions may be made. Keep the punches within the outline marks of the pattern.

Use a heavy hammer with repoussé tools to make deep impressions from the back.

❺ Heat the piece gently, holding it in insulated tweezers over the pitch bowl, until it is free of pitch. Anneal until all pitch residue disappears. If the repousséd areas are fairly deep, it is a good idea to fill them with pitch and allow it to harden before returning the piece topside up into the pitch. Each time the metal is put into the pitch, the corners should be bent over to hold it firm. The top is then worked with the chasing tools to give the desired decorative surface. The edges and the background of the pattern are flattened with smooth, flat punches, or punches with a pattern engraved into them.

Use the flat end of the hammer with the chasing tool to make the indent for the line on the front of the work.

SAMPLES • **Chasing and repoussé**

This unique form of surface decoration is used to create complex and very detailed pictures, or simply to raise the form from the back of the piece. Perfecting the technique requires a little time and patience, but the end results make the effort worthwhile. Most of the samples shown here are not too difficult and can be achieved reasonably quickly, although the masks and pictures will take a little longer.

HOW THE SAMPLES WERE ACHIEVED

SUBSTRATE 1-4

SILVER

❶ The square for the pattern was marked on the back and oblong and round-ended repoussé punches were used alternately. The edges of the metal were then flattened from the front.

❷ The main pattern was achieved with repoussé punches used from the back. Chasing tools were used from the front to define the lines of the pattern, and a matting tool was used to flatten and define the background.

❸ The pattern was drawn on the front and back of the piece. A straight-faced repoussé punch was used to impress the pattern. A flat repoussé punch was used on the front (rather than on the back as is usual in repoussé work) to flatten in between.

❹ Silver was passed through a rolling mill with thick fabric. The letters were scribed in reverse on the back and a chasing tool used to outline the letters and push them through to the front.

SUBSTRATE 5-6

COPPER

❺ The piece was first heated to achieve a good color, annealed, and worked with repoussé punches to produce the central pattern. It was heated again and reshaped into a soft dome with large, round punches.

❻ Decreasing circles were scribed onto the reverse, and worked with a chasing tool to define the lines and push them to the front. A round-ended repoussé punch was used between the lines on the front to create the final shape.

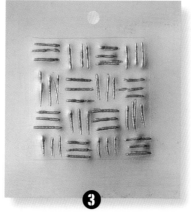

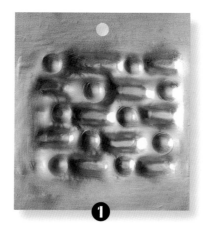

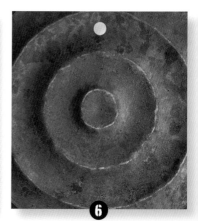

HELPFUL HINTS

- The ideal thickness of metal for repoussé work is approximately 0.6mm. If it is too thin, you risk breaking it; if it is too thick, it is difficult to work with.
- You will feel the metal hardening quite quickly as you work it. Anneal it at regular intervals to keep it soft.

- After the piece has been placed in the pitch, allow the pitch to cool completely before starting to work on it. If the pitch is still warm, the metal will sink deeper and deeper into it, making working difficult.
- Make sure that the lines to be followed are clear on both the front and the back of the piece.

SUBSTRATE 7-9

COPPER

7 The pattern was traced on both sides of the metal and worked equally back and front with several annealings to keep the surface soft. It was finished with a brass brush and liquid soap.

8 The man's face was repousséd out and the detail worked from the front with chasing tools. The leaf area was only slightly repousséd, being mainly worked flat from the front.

9 The background areas of this piece were flattened from the front. Round-ended repoussé punches in different sizes were worked from the back to produce the intricate design.

SUBSTRATE 10-11

GILDING METAL

10 The outline was transferred onto the back with a chasing tool and the detail worked alternately from back to front. The front detail was achieved with fine chasing tools and the difference in height and depth achieved from the back with repoussé punches.

11 Very fine chasing tools were used as in sample 10 to create the wood effect.

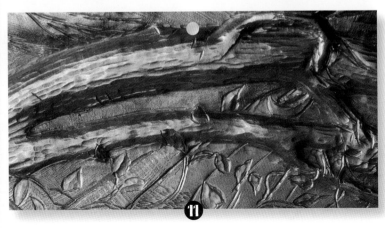

These pieces demonstrate the enormous range of finishes that can be achieved with chasing and repoussé. The beautifully smooth finish on the earrings and necklace provides a strong contrast with the fine detail on the box lids. The wheel earrings are deceptively simple in appearance; by retaining the punch markings, a handmade, timeless quality is achieved.

SHELL EARRINGS

Harriet St Leger • Sterling silver and 18-carat gold
The decorative gold bands and dots on these shelllike earrings accentuate the form and volume that has been created by repoussé.

JEWELRY BOX

Julian Stevens • Silver-plated gilding metal
This delicate image has been first chased from the front, then repousséd, and then chased again.

TEARDROPS NECKLACE

Harriet St Leger • Sterling silver
and 18-carat gold
*Three repousséd teardrop shapes
with gold decoration have been
threaded on a chain for a
very wearable piece.*

GARNET PENDANT

Harriet St Leger • Sterling silver and garnet
*This intricate repoussé shaping has been formed
into a pendant and set with a garnet for a piece
reminiscent of jewelry from the Art Nouveau era.*

WHEEL EARRINGS

Jonathan Swan • 18-carat yellow gold
*Repoussé has been used to form
a striking yet simple design for these
earrings, which emphasize the sculptural
qualities this technique can produce.*

Abrasives The natural or man-made sand-like particles used to smooth or clean away marks on a surface, as can be found adhered to abrasive papers.

Alloy A mixture of metals.

Arkansas stone A smooth stone usually used for sharpening tools.

Annealing The process of softening metals using heat. Most non-ferrous metals can be softened by heating them to dull red and allowing them to cool.

Ball-pein hammer A hammer with one round face and one flat face. The round "ball" end is used for shaping metal.

Borax A flux used by jewelers that usually comes in the form of a solid cone that must be ground with water in a small ceramic dish to form a paste.

Brass An alloy of copper and zinc. It is usually yellow in color.

Brass brush A wheel-shaped brush with brass wire bristles, used for cleaning and surface-finishing items made from gold, silver, copper, or brass.

Bronze A pale yellow metal used for casting that is generally an alloy of copper and tin.

Bullion Gold and silver.

Burnish To polish by rubbing.

Burnisher A highly-polished tool of steel or agate which is rubbed against softer metal to harden it and also to impart a polish.

Burr A rough edge created by filing or drilling metal. This must be removed with care to avoid scratching the surrounding area.

Carat A measure of the fineness of gold or gold alloy. The number of carats is the number of parts by weight of pure gold in 24 parts of the metal. Pure gold is therefore described as 24-carat, and 14-carat is an alloy that contains 14 parts of pure gold in 24 parts of the alloy. Sometimes spelled karat.

Carborundum An industrial abrasive.

Casting The pouring of molten metal into a mold.

Chasing The process of marking a design in metal from the front.

Chasing hammer A hammer with a large face for striking chasing tools or flattening.

Chisel A metal tool with a cutting edge.

Copper A reddish-colored, malleable, ductile metal.

Crucible A heat-proof vessel in which metal and other substances requiring a high degree of heat are molton.

Enameling The fusion of a transparent or opaque vitreous substance to the surface of metal, glass, or pottery.

Engraving The process of cutting away the surface of a substance, using a sharp steel tool called a graver. Lines are often engraved in a metal surface to form a decoration or inscription.

Etching The controlled corrosion of a surface using acids to create decorative or textured patterns.

Etch resist Used to protect or mask areas that are not to be etched so that pattern and detail can be formed.

Ferrous metal Containing iron.

Finish A term used to describe the cleaning up of a piece by sanding and polishing.

Firescale The copper content in standard silver, sometimes revealed when silver is heated.

Flux The generic term used to describe a chemical used as an antioxidant as part of the soldering process.

Fusing The joining of metals by means of heat without the use of solder. The metals being joined melt, but only on the surface.

Fly press A type of screw press used for pressing, punching, and forging.

Gilding metal An alloy of copper and zinc. Its color resembles that of gold.

Glass brush A brush made with fine glass fibers used for cleaning metal.

Gold The metal most commonly associated with jewelry. It is naturally found as a rich yellow color although it can be alloyed to be white, red, or green in color.

Granulation The decoration or texturing of a surface by the application of tiny balls (grains) of gold or silver.

Graver See Engraving.

Gum arabic A gum obtained from several species of the acacia tree, especially *Acacia senegal* and *A. arabica*, and used in the manufacture of adhesives and ink, as well as in food production. It contains arabinose, galactose, rhamnose, and glucuronic acid, and is completely soluble in hot or cold water, yielding a viscous solution.

Gum tragacanth A gum obtained as a dried exudate from various Asiatic and Eastern European plants of the genus *Astragalus*, especially *A. gummifer*. It consists of bassorin and tragacanthin, and swells in water to form a gel.

Hammer A tool for beating or striking metal.

Hydrofluoric acid A solution of hydrogen fluoride in water used for etching glass and enamel. Corrosive and highly poisonous.

Inlay A decorative technique where one material is inserted into the surface of another in a pattern or outline.

Jade oil Jade oil is used to stabilize and maintain metal coloring. It retards tarnishing by depositing a thin layer of resin on the metal.

Lead cake A block of lead used to support metal while it is being hammered.

Malleability The quality of metal that makes it capable of being hammered or rolled permanently out of shape, without breaking or cracking. Most non-ferrous metals are malleable, gold being the most malleable metal of all.

Mica A group of glass-like minerals that break easily into thin layers or sheets and are not damaged by heat.

Mordant A corrosive solution used in etching.

Oxidation A term generally applied to the chemical reaction of a substance with oxygen or an oxygen-containing material which adds oxygen atom(s) to the compound being oxidized. Some common forms of oxidation are the tarnishing of silver and the rusting of iron.

Paillon Term for pieces of solder, taken from the French word "flake"

Patination A process for coloring metals through exposure to a variety of chemicals.

Pendant motor A tool used in engraving.

Photoetching A form of etching that uses ultraviolet light to expose artwork on to sensitised metal sheets that are then etched.

Pickle A caustic solution used for removing oxides and borax from the surface of metals, particularly after soldering operations. It is usually used warm.

Pickling A process that uses a chemical solution to remove the black oxide layer that results from heating and soldering.

Planishing Polishing or flattening by hammering with a mirror-finished hammer face.

Piercing The technique of sawing patterns and shapes from metal sheet.

Piercing saw A saw with a blade narrow enough to be threaded through a drilled hole so that a pattern can be cut out from sheet metal or other material.

Pitch A mixture of bitumen, plaster, and wax used in chasing and repoussé.

Pumice powder A powdered form of volcanic rock used with water to abrade and clean the surface of metals.

Punch A tool (usually steel), variously shaped at one end for different uses, and either solid, for stamping or perforating holes, or hollow and sharp-edged, for cutting out blanks in metal and other substances.

Quench Dropping hot metal straight into water, or a mixture of oil and water, for rapid cooling and hardening.

Repoussé The modeling of sheet metal using hammers and punches. The metal is fixed to a yielding surface and work is carried out on both back and front.

Reticulation A surface treatment where controlled heating of the metal (usually gold or silver) results in a rippled, molten effect.

Rolling mill A tool used to reduce the thickness of sheets of metal. Smooth steel rollers encased in a cast iron frame reduce thickness, a little at a time, with each reduction of the gap between the rollers.

Scribe A pointed tool used for marking or scoring lines in metalworking.

Silver A light gray metal that is malleable and ductile.

Solder A fusible alloy for joining metals. The different grades of solder (hard, medium, easy) indicate the temperature at which the solder melts.

Hard solder melts at high temperatures; easy solder melts at low temperatures.

Soldering The joining of metals by means of heat, using silver-based alloys.

Sprue The channel through which molten metal flows into the mold during the casting process.

Stamping The process of forming a pattern in sheet metal, using a punch bearing the complete design. The pattern is formed by a single blow and the process is suitable for mass production.

Steel A gray ferrous metal often used for tool making.

Stop-out fluid An acid-resistant medium used in etching.

Tempering The process of heating ferrous metal after hardening to reduce its brittleness.

Tool steel Carbon and alloy steels that are particularly well-suited to being made into tools. Their suitability comes from their distinct toughness, resistance to abrasion, and their ability to hold a cutting edge.

Water of Ayr stone A fine abrasive stone.

Wet-and-dry papers Abrasive papers that may be used either wet or dry, ranging in grades of abrasiveness from 220 (coarse) through 400, 600, 800 up to 1200 (very fine and used just before polishing).

Zinc A white metal mainly used as a constituent of brass and other alloys.

ACKNOWLEDGMENTS

For Steve: 1604-2004

Many thanks indeed to Linda Lewin for her invaluable contribution in sharing her organic glue granulation technique on page 87.

Thanks to Jean Scott-Moncrieff for the loan of some press forming patterns.

My special thanks also to Paul and Laura for making the photography fun, Sam Le Prevost for all his help in the workshop, Jo Fisher for her patience and help, and a big thanks to all the jewelers whose work appears in the book, for taking the time to supply photographs and technical information and sharing the wealth of inspiration in their work.

PHOTOGRAPHERS

Sven Berggreen (Geometric earrings, p.49) **Mike Blissett** (Fused gold necklace, p.18; Geometric necklace, p.27; Double spiral, p.32; Screw-top pendants, p.38; Deviation earrings, p.39; Doughnut pendants, p.40; Spiral necklace, p.49; Pendants, p.51; Line-dot necklace, p.116; Double musical rings, p.117) **Graham Clark** (Sundrops necklace, p.85) **Anthony Cook** (Pompom rings, pp.5, 66) **Joël Degen** (Orbit necklace, p.45; Hollow shapes collection, p.48; Japan earrings/brooches, pp.12, 50; Patterned bracelet, p.50; Spirals brooch, p.51; Rondelle necklace, p.59; Strip earrings, p.113; Palladium pendant and earrings, p.117) **Brian Fischbacher** (Pollen brooch, p.91; Stems brooch, p.92) **Jeppe Gudmundsen Holmgreen** (Patterned rings, p.25; Spiral patterned rings, pp.4, 5, 26) **David Harban** (Gray target pendant, p.100) **Huw Jones** (Cracked dome necklace, p.78) **Robert Kirchstein** (Patterned bangles, pp.7, 32; Curved bangle, p.79) **Graham Mathers** (*Cofio*/Remember II, p.38; *Gwynt Yr Hwyr*/The Evening Breeze, p.50; Carved collection, p.67; *Eifionydd* collection, pp.9, 100, 101, 125) **Elizabeth Olver** (Price tag bracelet, p.109) **Kuniyasu Usui** (Five bangles, p.58; Wire ring, p.12, 59; Twig pendants, p.67; Twig bangle, p.85; Cloisonné brooch, p.101; Corded pendant, p.101)

While every effort has been made to credit contributors, Quarto would like to apologize should there have been any omissions or errors—and would be pleased to make the appropriate correction for future editions of the book.

All other photographs and illustrations are the copyright of Quarto Publishing plc.

FURTHER READING

Basic Jewelry Making Techniques, Jinks McGrath (Krause Publications, US, 2003; A&C Black, UK, 2004)

The Colouring, Bronzing & Patinating of Metals, Richard Hughes and Michael Rowe (Watson-Guptill Publications, 1991)

The Complete Metalsmith, Tim McCreight (Sterling Publishing, 1991)

The Design and Creation of Jewellery, Robert von Neumann (Chilton Book Company, 2003)

The Encyclopedia of Jewelry Making Techniques, Jinks McGrath (Running Press, US, 1995; Headline, UK, 1995)

Jewelry Concepts and Technology, Oppi Untracht (Trafalgar Square, 1996)

Silverwork & Jewellery, H. Wilson (John Hogg, 1912)

Traditional Jewelry of India, Oppi Untracht (Harry N. Abrams, 1997)